Parent Letters for the Primary Grades

Adapted from *The Learning Letter,* Morton Malkofsky Publishing
Editor: Joellyn Thrall Cicciarelli
Illustrator: Catherine Yuh
Project Director: Carolea Williams

CTP ©1997 Creative Teaching Press, Inc., Cypress, CA 90630

Table of Contents

Introduction

Parent Letters for the Primary Grades are designed to strengthen the home-school connection and reinforce learning at home. The letters offer parents meaningful parent/child activities in the core subject areas of reading, math, language arts, social studies, and science.

A *Did You Know?* section is included at the top of each letter to explain why an activity is important and provide background in the activity's subject area. Sections are written in easy-to-understand language, free from educational jargon.

A *How You Can Help* section explains each parent/child activity. Activities are designed as a fun way to support what is being taught in school.

Reproducibles follow specific activities throughout the book. Send each reproducible home with its corresponding parent letter.

When working with parent letters, consider the following suggestions.

- Send activities that support currently-taught units. With simultaneous home/school learning, students receive the reinforcement they need to make ideas "stick."

- Send letters home on brightly-colored paper so they will be noticed. Inform parents of the color so they can watch for them.

- Provide a parent-letter support system. Invite parents to call or write when they have questions about an activity.

- During the first week of school, send home the Welcome Back letter and an activity letter as homework. (If children feel the first one is required, they will be more likely to try it, like it, and beg for more!)

- Send home a group of letters just before vacation as an activity packet.

- Write your own letters to reinforce ideas specific to your curriculum. Keep them with this book for reuse.

- Laminate previously-sent letters and keep them in a central location. Check the letters out so students can repeat favorites again and again.

Dear Parents,

Welcome to a new school year! Your child is about to embark on an exciting learning adventure—and you can come along! Throughout the year, you will receive letters that provide important information and fun activities to help your child with reading, math, language arts, social studies, and science.

You can recognize these letters by their format. There is a *Did You Know?* section that offers an explanation of why the activity is important and background in the activity's subject area. The second section is called *How You Can Help*. This section explains a parent/child activity through clear, easy-to-follow directions.

Try each activity as you receive it. If you don't have time to do an activity right away, keep the letter for later use. Activities are designed to be used by you and your child, but many can be completed as a family.

You may wish to keep the letters in a three-ring binder. That way, you can invite your child to choose favorite or new activities to do during vacation or after the school year ends.

Try one activity and you'll try them all. They're quick, easy, and best of all, an opportunity to spend special time with your child.

Sincerely,

Parent Letters for the Primary Grades © 1997 Creative Teaching Press

Dear Parents,

Did You Know?

Your child can become a better student by becoming a better "homeworker." Homework offers important reviewing and learning time away from the classroom, helping your child become a more independent learner. To help your child get the most from homework, try the following tips—your child may actually start looking forward to it!

How You Can Help

1. Help your child find a special quiet place to study. It may be the bedroom, basement, or attic—it doesn't matter where, as long as he or she will not be disturbed.

2. Provide your child with the materials he or she needs to complete the work, such as paper, pencils, pens, crayons, markers, or other special supplies.

3. Set a schedule. Have your child work for 30 minutes a day whether homework is assigned or not. A routine will become a habit. (If no homework is assigned, have your child read or work on an art project for 30 minutes.)

4. Show your child samples of his or her neatest work. Explain that homework should meet this neatness standard.

5. When your child has trouble, help him or her without giving answers. Instead, give clues such as *Reread the third sentence to find the answer. The question asks for the total. Does that mean the numbers all together or only the number left over?*

6. Help your child think like a teacher. When doing assignments, have your child ask him- or herself, *What should students remember? What are the most important ideas and facts? What are the steps needed to solve this problem?*

7. When studying for a test, show your child how to create a "fake test" with questions and answers written just like the teacher's. Do the test with your child.

8. For spelling tests, have your child create flash cards each week. Invite your child to quiz you as well as be quizzed.

Dear Parents,

It's been a great year, and I hope these letters have been a big part of the success.

Letter activities can be used again and again—so pull them out over vacation. Try these suggestions to make vacation activities more meaningful.

- Invite your child to choose activities, whether old favorites or new ones.
- To keep activities interesting, vary subject area each day. For example, do a reading activity on Monday, science on Tuesday, math on Wednesday, language arts on Thursday, and social studies on Friday.
- After each activity, go to the library and challenge your child to discover more about the activity's subject.
- Have an activity day. Invite several of your child's friends to participate in a day of letter-activity fun.
- Get the whole family involved—complete activities together.

Have a wonderful vacation!

Sincerely,

Parent Letters for the Primary Grades © 1997 Creative Teaching Press

Dear Parents,

Did You Know?

Your child experiences more than a fun time when you read aloud to him or her. As you read, your child makes the connection between the spoken and written word, learns new vocabulary, and sees good reading techniques. A great way to demonstrate good reading techniques as you read aloud is to use "echo reading." Try the following echo-reading activity, and watch your child go!

How You Can Help

1. Choose a book both you and your child will enjoy.

2. Place your child on your lap or in front of you.

3. Position your mouth directly behind one of his or her ears.

4. Invite your child to read the book aloud with you. As you read, whisper each word into his or her ear (at a regular reading pace), allowing your child to read aloud and echo your words. Your child's "echoes" should occur at (or at almost) the same time as your original reading.

5. Use "echo reading" whenever your child wants to read a difficult or new book to you.

Dear Parents,

Did You Know?

One of the best ways to help your child learn reading skills is to read aloud to him or her. Reading aloud and talking about books helps your child understand stories and make sense of words. As you read aloud, your child "makes pictures" in his or her head, imagining the story in action. Your child's vocabulary will grow as he or she hears new, exciting words and ideas. Try reading aloud to your child—it's easy, fun, and educational!

How You Can Help

1. Choose a book both you and your child will enjoy.

2. Read the title and discuss the cover illustration. Have your child guess what the book will be about by looking at the cover.

3. Read the book aloud. As you read, discuss pictures, new vocabulary, and interesting events.

4. Before reading the end of the story, invite your child to predict what will happen.

5. After reading, ask him or her to name a main character, event, problem, or solution in the story.

6. Invite your child to find and share his or her favorite part of the story. Reread that part aloud.

Parent Letters for the Primary Grades ©1997 Creative Teaching Press

Dear Parents,

Did You Know?

If you make reading aloud fun, your child will learn to love reading and want to read on his or her own. When reading is fun, time passes quickly and everyone is left begging for one more story. One great way to make read-aloud time fun is to become an "actor" and read a story as if it were a play. Use the following activity to put some drama into your reading.

How You Can Help

1. Choose a book with interesting characters and a lively plot. If you need help finding books, consult a children's librarian.

2. Practice reading the story to yourself first. Use low, high, loud, and soft voices to show exciting or scary parts. Invent funny accents for each character.

3. Choose a quiet time to read—a time when you will not be interrupted and your child is not busy.

4. Read the story aloud with expression, using the voices and accents you invented.

Parent Letters for the Primary Grades ©1997 Creative Teaching Press

Dear Parents,

Did You Know?

Everything, including reading, is more fun when you experience it as a family. Reading as a family is one of the best ways to encourage a child to read. Your child will become a life-long reader if he or she observes the family reading and enjoys reading with them. To create family reading time, use the following activity.

How You Can Help

1. Set aside a special time and day in which each member of the family reads something aloud. (Young children have short attention spans. If your family is large, have family members take turns on different evenings.)

2. Shut off televisions and radios.

3. Take the telephone off the hook, or have an answering machine take calls.

4. Invite each family member to read aloud a book, newspaper or magazine article, cartoon, recipe, or other reading selection.

5. As a family, discuss each selection.

Parent Letters for the Primary Grades ©1997 Creative Teaching Press

Dear Parents,

Did You Know?

Family outings can turn into terrific reading adventures. When your child experiences educational places or events, he or she becomes curious about their subjects. For example, if you take your child to see a dinosaur exhibit at the Museum of Natural History, he or she will want to know more about dinosaurs—time to stock your shelves with dinosaur books! Children love to read about anything that interests them, so whet their reading appetites with a family field trip.

How You Can Help

1. Plan field trips in advance. Consider trips to museums, historical sites, zoos, or botanical gardens.

2. Collect information about each place. Consult the newspaper for upcoming events such as dance, puppet, theater, arts and crafts, or musical performances. Visit a library or bookstore to find information about museums and historical sites. Pick up pamphlets at a nearby hotel that advertise zoos, gardens, and other places of interest.

3. Copy the information and place it in a folder.

4. Once a month, invite your child to choose a place to visit. Take the information from the folder and read it aloud.

5. Go on the field trip. After touring, ask your child his or her favorite part of the trip.

6. Collect books about a subject from the trip your child found most interesting. Read the books aloud to your child. If questions arise, search for answers as you read.

Dear Parents,

Did You Know?

When your child can hear the beginning sound in a word (such as the *b* sound in *bat*), he or she is on the way to better reading. With this hearing skill, your child will soon look at difficult words, name all their sounds, and put the sounds together to read. Playing with beginning sounds is a perfect way to help your child gain good reading skills. Try this fun, easy activity to get started.

How You Can Help

1. Write letters of the alphabet on individual paper slips or old business cards.

2. Place the letters in a paper bag.

3. Have your child pull a letter from the bag.

4. Ask your child to think of a silly two-word phrase that starts with the same sound, such as *purple penguins, dancing doorknobs,* or *hiccuping hippos.*

5. Now it's your turn—choose a letter and make up a phrase.

6. Take turns until you've used all the letters.

Parent Letters for the Primary Grades ©1997 Creative Teaching Press

Dear Parents,

Did You Know?

Hearing sounds is an important part of reading. When your child can hear beginning, middle, and ending sounds in words, he or she is ready to read, write, and spell. For example, when your child can hear the *c, a,* and *t* sounds in *cat,* he or she can probably read, write, and spell the word with just a little practice. Use the following activity to give your child some fun sound/hearing practice.

How You Can Help

1. Gather several magazines and large sheets of newsprint or other blank paper.

2. Choose a sound you want your child to hear, such as the *b* sound. If your child is a beginning reader, have him or her listen for the sound at the beginning of words. If your child is a more advanced reader, have him or her listen for the sound at the middle or end of words.

3. Invite your child to go through the magazines and cut out pictures with that sound at the beginning, middle, or end. For example, if you want to focus on the *b* sound, your child might cut out a picture of a baby.

4. Paste the pictures on the paper.

5. If your child becomes restless after pasting two or three pictures, stop and continue the activity at a later date, or have him or her look for the sound at the end of words.

6. After each pasting session, say the picture names. Emphasize the sound in the words and say them together aloud.

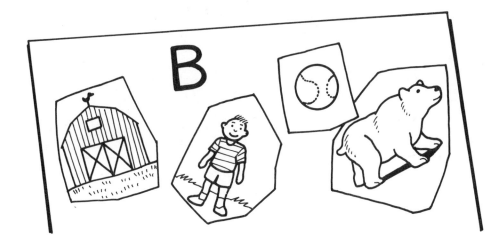

Dear Parents,

Did You Know?

Dr. Seuss knew how to get children to read—make the words rhyme! Children love reading rhymes, but rhymes are more than fun. They help children pay attention to, see, and hear sounds in words. When children know sounds, they are better able to put them together to read. Help your child become a better reader by playing the following rhyming game.

How You Can Help

1. Play this game anywhere—in the car, when doing chores, or when taking a walk.

2. Suggest a word such as *bear,* and invite your child to name a word that rhymes with it, such as *hair, care,* or *dare.*

3. Take turns naming words until you cannot think of any more.

4. Choose another word and play the game again.

5. To vary the game, make up a verse from two rhyming words, such as *I saw a bear with purple hair.* Give two or three examples and then ask your child to think of a verse.

6. Help your child write the verse on drawing paper, and invite him or her to illustrate it.

Parent Letters for the Primary Grades ©1997 Creative Teaching Press

Dear Parents,

Did You Know?

Hearing all sounds in a word—beginning, middle, and ending—is important for reading. For your child to "sound out" a new or difficult word, he or she must know ending as well as beginning sounds. Since ending sounds do not stand out when people talk and are harder to hear, we must help children pay attention to them. Use the following activity to help your child listen for ending sounds in words.

How You Can Help

1. Say a sentence pattern with an object at the end, such as *I went on a trip and took a hair dryer.* As you name the object, emphasize the ending sound (*/r/* in *hair dryer*). Ask your child to listen for the very last sound you said (*/r/*).

2. Invite your child to repeat the sentence and complete it with the name of new object that begins with the last sound, such as *I went on a trip and took a rubber band.*

3. Take turns until you run out of logical ideas. At that point, change the words to silly objects, such as *I went on a trip and took a meatloaf.* Or, change the whole sentence. Sentences could be changed to *I went to the zoo and saw a . . . , I went to the market and bought a . . . ,* or *I went to the beach and saw a . . . .*

Phonemic Awareness and Phonics

Dear Parents,

Did You Know?

Some sounds cannot be described by naming just one letter because they are made by putting together two or more letters, such as *ch* in *chair*, *sh* in *shirt*, or *th* in *that*. To help your child hear, "sound out," and read words with two- and three-letter combinations, call attention to them when reading aloud, help your child sound them out, or have your child "play" with them. The following game is one way your child can play with and learn sound combinations.

How You Can Help

1. Cut out the attached Sound Wheelie or make one of your own (see illustration).

2. Pull a paper clip slightly open and push the point through the center of the wheelie to make a spinner.

3. Have your child spin the spinner. When it stops, say the sound of the letter combination on which he or she landed, such as /ch/.

4. If your child is a beginning reader, ask him or her to name a word that begins with that sound. For example, If you say /ch/, your child might say *chain*.

5. If your child is an advanced reader, have him or her say a word that ends with the chosen sound. For example, if you say /ch/, your child might say *bunch*.

6. To make the activity more challenging, have your child name words that have the sound at both the beginning and end.

Parent Letters for the Primary Grades ©1997 Creative Teaching Press

Sound Wheelie

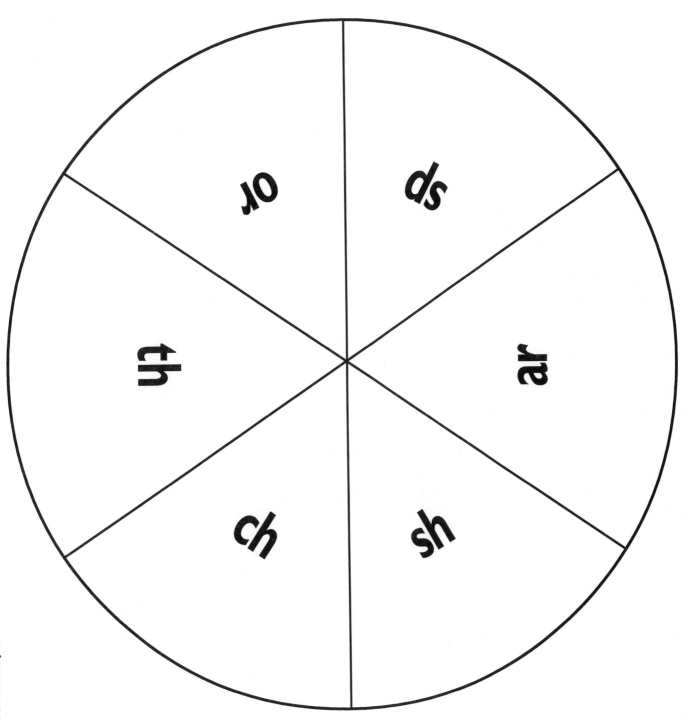

Dear Parents,

Did You Know?

Working with rhyming words helps children see and hear word similarities. When children see how words relate, they use this knowledge to "sound out" words when reading. Help your child see and hear how words relate by completing the following rhyming-word activity.

How You Can Help

1. Gather 26 small bathroom tiles, old business cards, or paper scraps to make game pieces. Write a letter of the alphabet on each piece. (If your child is an advanced reader, make two alphabets. The advanced game requires duplicated letters.)

2. If your child is a beginning reader, build a short word such as *at* with game pieces. Add a *c* to make the word *cat*. Read the word aloud.

3. Have your child explain how the word *cat* is like and different from *at*.

4. Remove the *c* from *cat* and ask your child to replace it with another letter to make a new word such as *bat, sat,* or *fat*. Invite your child to say the newly-formed word. (Accept invented, nonsense words as long as they rhyme.)

5. Take turns until all letters are used.

6. If your child is an advanced reader, complete the activity with more difficult words, and invite your child to build rhyming words spelled differently from the original word, such as *repeat, feet, treat, conceit,* or *complete*. Have your child point out spelling similarities and differences after making each word.

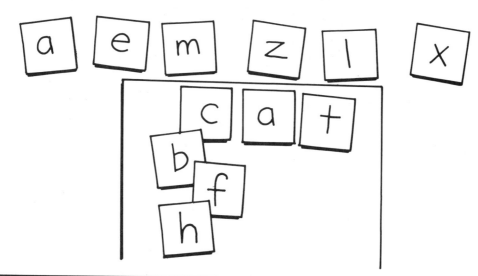

Parent Letters for the Primary Grades © 1997 Creative Teaching Press

Dear Parents,

Did You Know?

With a few clues and a little encouragement, most children can "sound out" and read new or difficult words. There are several easy ways to give your child clues rather than reading a word for him or her. Try the following clue suggestions as you read with your child—soon you will be creating your own!

How You Can Help

1. Use a popsicle stick as your child reads to you.

2. Listen to your child read. When he or she hesitates or stops at an unknown word, give one or more of the following clues:

    ● Use beginning-sound clues such as *This word begins like* picnic.

    ● Use rhyming-word clues such as *This word sounds like* bear, *but it begins with a* p *sound.*

    ● Cover the end of the word with the popsicle stick and give clues such as *I made part of the word disappear. What letters are left? What sounds do they make?*

    ● Cover the beginning of the word with the popsicle stick and give clues such as *I made the rest of the word disappear. What sounds do those letters make?* (Remove the popsicle stick.) *Now, let's put the sounds together. What does the whole word say?*

Phonemic Awareness and Phonics

Dear Parents,

Did You Know?

The more your child plays with words and sounds, the better reader he or she will become. Playing with beginning letters and sounds is one of the easiest ways to build your child's reading vocabulary. Whether your child is a new or experienced reader, he or she will benefit from playing the following sound/word game.

How You Can Help

1. If your child is a beginning reader, play the game with only two or three familiar letters. If your child is an advanced reader, play the game with beginning, middle, and ending letter combinations such as *ch, sh, tr, thr, ei, igh,* or *aim.*

2. Print a letter or letter combination on individual paper scraps or old business cards. Make at least 20 letter cards.

3. Shuffle the cards and place them face down on a table.

4. Invite your child to turn over the first card.

5. Have your child name a word that starts with that letter (or contains that letter combination) in 30 seconds or less.

6. If your child names a word, invite him or her to keep the card. If he or she cannot name a word, have him or her place the card in a new pile on the table.

7. Take turns until all cards in the first pile have been played. Play with the second pile to give your child a second chance to name words.

8. Have your child count his or her cards when finished. Keep score, and invite your child to beat his or her score the next time you play.

Parent Letters for the Primary Grades ©1997 Creative Teaching Press

Dear Parents,

Did You Know?

Whenever a learning reader reads, he or she stumbles over, misreads, asks about, and has trouble remembering "hard words." Hard words are usually words that cannot be "sounded out" easily, such as *recipe* or *bouquet*. To help your learning reader make "hard words" easy, try the following activity.

How You Can Help

1. Each time your child reads to you, write down one or two "hard words" on the left side of a list similar to that in the illustration.

2. Once a month, invite your child to try to read each word on the *Words I Want to Learn* side.

3. Have him or her talk about each word by answering one or more of the following questions:
   What does each word look like?
   What letter does each word begin with?
   What are some other words that begin that way?
   What letter does each word end with?
   What are the sounds that make up each word?
   What are some rhyming words for that word?

4. Help your child think of clues to remember the words. For example, tell him or her the word *why* can be remembered by saying the name of its last letter.

5. When your child reads a word without help, invite him or her to cross it off the *Words I Want to Learn* side and write it on the *Now I Know It!* side.

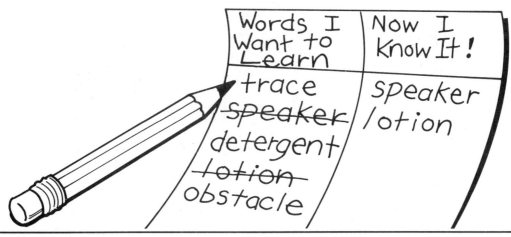

Dear Parents,

Did You Know?

When your child tries to read words not easily sounded out, such as *shoe,* he or she can become discouraged and give up. An important part of becoming a good reader is being a self-confident risk-taker when trying to read new or difficult words. Help your child take reading risks by playing the following wild-word game—your child will wrangle and tame those hard-to-read words!

How You Can Help

1. Gather a shoe box, scissors, plastic wrap, and tape.

2. Have your child use the materials to make a "wild-word cage."

3. Whenever your child reads aloud to you, write words with which he or she needs help on individual index cards. These are "wild words." Place the wild words in a container. Each week, have your child practice reading them.

4. Each time your child is able to read a wild word without help, invite him or her to put the word in the wild-word cage. Keep the rest of the wild words "on the loose" in the container, having your child try to read them each week until he or she can "cage" them.

5. Once a month, let the wild words escape from the cage and invite your child to read them again. Any words he or she misses should be placed back in the "on-the-loose" container for more practice.

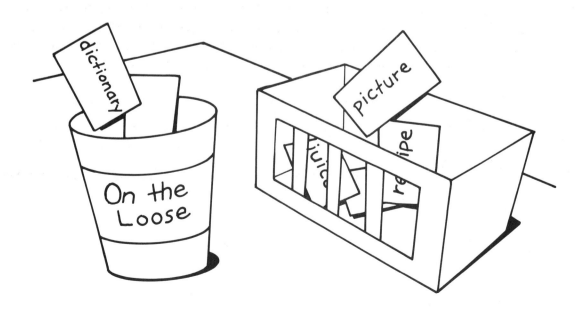

Parent Letters for the Primary Grades ©1997 Creative Teaching Press

Dear Parents,

Did You Know?

When your child can figure out a new word in a sentence by reading the words around it, he or she has gained a very important reading skill. For example, if your child can figure out the word *guests* by reading *There were seven _____ at my birthday party,* he or she is learning to decode words in context. Use the following activity to help your child figure out new words by reading around them.

How You Can Help

1. Using an index card for each word, write a sentence with a hard-to-read word. Hide the sentence from your child.

2. Write two other words that, when placed in the difficult word's place, would not make sense. For example, for the sentence, *I bought milk at the store,* you might make cards that read *ran* and *jumped* to replace the word *bought.*

3. Lay out the sentence, leaving out the missing word (and its replacements). Invite your child to read the sentence and think about words that would make sense in the space.

4. Lay out the three word choices. Have your child consider each word and guess which one fits in the sentence.

5. Repeat the activity with several different sentences and difficult words.

6. To vary the game, change the original sentence to follow the first sentence pattern. For example, if the original sentence was *We will go swimming when it gets warm,* the second sentence might be *We will go shopping when it stops raining.* By rereading the same words and word patterns, your child receives rereading practice that will help him or her remember the words every time he or she sees them.

Word Recognition

Dear Parents,

Did You Know?

The best teachers have known it for years—when you take the work out of reading "hard words," children don't think of them as hard. When reading is seen as fun instead of work, even the most reluctant reader becomes enthusiastic. Help your child enjoy learning "hard words" by trying a variation of an all-time favorite—checkers.

How You Can Help

1. Write new or hard words on several small sticky notes.

2. Place the sticky notes on the red spaces of a checkerboard.

3. Make another set of sticky notes with easy words (words your child can read), and cover the black spaces with these words.

4. When playing checkers, have your child read a sticky-note word before landing on that space. If your child needs help, read the word with him or her.

5. Take turns reading and moving checkers until someone wins the game.

Parent Letters for the Primary Grades ©1997 Creative Teaching Press

Dear Parents,

Did You Know?

How a word is shaped is a clue to how a word is spelled. Some words have tall letters (such as *tall*), some have short letters (such as *cream*), and some have letters with tails (such as *yesterday*). Each word's unique shape can be your child's reminder of its pronunciation and spelling. When you teach your child to notice and remember how words look, you've given him or her one more way to learn to read. Try the following activity to help your child get new words "into shape."

How You Can Help

1. Choose a few words your child needs to practice and write them on lined paper.

2. Invite your child to choose a word and trace around the letters to make an oddly-shaped box.

3. Encourage your child to notice which letters are tall, short, and have tails.

4. Ask your child to describe the letter shapes, telling which are round, slanted, have dots, or only straight lines.

5. Next to the word, draw the shape your child has drawn and have your child write the letters inside in the correct place.

6. Repeat the activity with the other words.

7. To vary the activity, choose words that are objects, such as *cake* or *tree*. Have your child draw the objects around the words after he or she writes inside your shapes.

Dear Parents,

Did You Know?

Newspapers offer an inexpensive, fun way to help your child with reading. Most kids love the comics, entertainment, and sports sections. Even headlines, advertisements, and the classified section can offer hours of reading fun. Make the most of your newspaper by using the following read-all-about-it activity.

How You Can Help

1. For beginning readers, scan the newspaper and make a list of two or three words your child uses every day, such as *baseball, computer,* or *water.* For advanced readers, find and write five or six words related to current events, such as *election, hurricane,* or *famine.*

2. Show your child each word.

3. Invite your child to scan the newspaper page by page to find the listed words.

4. When your child finds a word, have him or her circle it with a crayon and look for the next word.

5. After your child has found each word once, read each headline or sentence containing a chosen word and discuss the related news story.

6. When the activity is complete, discuss newspaper sections and why people read them.

Parent Letters for the Primary Grades ©1997 Creative Teaching Press

Dear Parents,

Did You Know?

Poems, songs, and nursery rhymes offer your child fun and much more! Silly subjects and rhyming words make poems, songs, and nursery rhymes perfect reading tools for beginning and advanced readers. Try the following poetic activity with your learning reader. He or she will beg to do it again and again!

How You Can Help

1. Write each word of a familiar poem, song, or nursery rhyme on a separate paper strip.

2. Lay the strips on a table, making a new row for each new line.

3. Read the lines aloud twice, and have your child point to each word as it is read.

4. Have your child close his or her eyes.

5. Mix up the words in the first line.

6. Invite your child to put the words in order.

7. Move down each line, mixing up words and having your child arrange them.

8. For a final round, mix up the entire poem, song, or nursery rhyme, shifting words into other lines. Challenge your child to put all the words in order.

Word Recognition

Dear Parents,

Did You Know?

Speaking, listening, reading, spelling, and writing all use words. So when you help your child read, you're also helping him or her learn to speak, listen, spell, and write. How wonderful that one activity can do so much! Help your child develop all these skills and more by playing an exciting version of Bingo.

How You Can Help

1. Have your child choose 16 words he or she wants to learn to read or spell. Words can be taken from books, favorite school subjects (such as plants or whales), or just about anywhere. Write each word on individual paper scraps.

2. Lay the words on a table so both you and your child can read them.

3. Prepare the attached Bingo cards by writing each word in a square in random order. Have your child do the same.

4. Use pennies, candy, or buttons for markers.

5. Gather and shuffle the word papers. Place them in a pile, face down.

6. Have your child be the "caller." Have him or her choose a word and read it aloud.

7. Place a marker over the word called. Have your child do the same.

8. The first player to cover one row (in any direction) calls, *Bingo!*

h○e	tape	mark	clip
train	pencil	bottle	boot
heart	golden	t○el	write
jealous	yel○w	scissors	ticket

yellow!

Parent Letters for the Primary Grades ©1997 Creative Teaching Press

Word Bingo

Word Recognition

Dear Parents,

Did You Know?

If you play secretary and take notes for your child as he or she dictates, you show him or her how speaking, listening, writing, and reading are related. You model correct spelling and grammar, and best of all, you show your child that what he or she says is important. Use paper or a computer to play secretary with your child whenever possible—the following activity will help you get started.

How You Can Help

1. Complete this activity over several days.

2. Gather an unfamiliar picture book, writing paper, and masking tape.

3. Cover all the words in the book with tape, leaving illustrations only.

4. Look through the book with your child, discussing characters, setting, and a possible plot.

5. Invite your child to make up words for the story by dictating them for each page.

6. Play secretary and record each word your child says.

7. Read the new story to your child. Then, have your child read it aloud to you.

8. Remove the masking tape and read the original story to see how close your child's story is to the original.

Parent Letters for the Primary Grades © 1997 Creative Teaching Press

Dear Parents,

Did You Know?

Funny ideas and stories are what keep many children interested in reading. If your child loves jokes and silly stories, provide him or her with lots of opportunities to read them. An inexpensive way to give your child something funny to read is to use newspaper comic strips. The following activity offers one way to use comics and is sure to give you ideas for many more!

How You Can Help

1. Read the newspaper comics section with your child.

2. Have your child cut out several speech bubbles with words he or she thinks are funny.

3. Have your child choose one of the speech bubbles to use in his or her own comic strip.

4. Invite your child to draw and write a new comic strip, gluing the chosen speech bubble in place.

5. Store extra clippings in an envelope for future projects such as additions to home-made greeting cards, photographs, or letters.

Dear Parents,

Did You Know?

Your child will be more motivated to read if he or she is reading something written by you! Children love to receive mail, and who better to send it than family members. Whether it's an "I'm-so-proud-of-you" letter for an advanced reader or a short surprise note for a beginning reader, your child will be excited to read.

How You Can Help

1. Each week, post two or three messages to your child in unusual but hard-to-miss places. Try the following ideas to get started.

2. Set an empty plate on the table with a note saying, *Look on the shelf by the window. Find the box and look inside. There are two surprises waiting for you.*

3. Place two treats in your child's coat pocket. With the treats, place a note that says, *Here's something for you and a friend.* Finally, pin a note on your child's coat that says, *Look in your pocket.*

4. Pin a note on a stray sock that says, *My twin is lost. If you find it, you will receive a reward.*

5. In your child's lunch box, place a note that says, *Congratulations. I'm so proud you won the spelling bee. I love you.*

Parent Letters for the Primary Grades ©1997 Creative Teaching Press

Dear Parents,

Did You Know?

Reading is understanding. If a child can pronounce long words but cannot understand them, he or she is not really reading. By talking about and playing with stories, you are helping your child understand words—the true meaning of reading. Try the following fun activity to help your child make meaning from a story.

How You Can Help

1. After your child has finished reading a book, discuss the story, including three important events.

2. Give your child a long strip of white paper and invite him or her to draw dividing lines to make three sections. Ask your child to illustrate one important story event in each section.

3. Staple or tape the strip together so it forms a ring.

4. Attach three pieces of string, ribbon, or yarn to the top of the ring. Gather the loose ends and tie them in a knot. Hang the knotted end from a light fixture or ceiling so the suspended Story-Go-Round can spin.

5. Invite your child to share his or her Story-Go-Round with family members.

Reading Comprehension

Dear Parents,

Did You Know?

An important part of reading is remembering the order in which things happen. When your child can use pictures and words to help him or her recall the order of story events, he or she is on the way to becoming a great reader. Help your child put stories in order by completing the following activity.

How You Can Help

1. Read the newspaper comics section.

2. Choose a comic strip your child enjoyed, cut out each frame, and number the back of each frame in order.

3. Mix up the frames. Have your child look at the pictures, reread each frame, and try to place the comic strip in order.

4. If the strip is placed in a different order, ask your child to explain the arrangement. Accept the order if it makes sense. If the order does not make sense, give your child clues to help him or her rearrange the strip.

5. Have your child check the numbers on the frame backs after arranging them.

6. For advanced readers, use long comic strips or remove a frame, inviting your child to put the strip back in order by making an educated guess about which frame is missing.

Parent Letters for the Primary Grades ©1997 Creative Teaching Press

Dear Parents,

Did You Know?

Picture and chapter books aren't the only books your child likes to read. Most children love to read informational books about real things and people such as dinosaurs, airplanes, inventors, holidays, or foreign countries. The key to getting your child to read informational books is to find subjects in which he or she is interested. Use the following activity to help your child become interested in reading nonfiction.

How You Can Help

1. Note your child's favorites such as favorite animals, food, clothing, or places. List his or her favorites on paper or a computer. Include all subjects, even unusual ones such as bicycles or sharks.

2. On your next visit to the library, bring the list and have your child look for books on one of the listed topics.

3. Update the list on a regular basis. (As your child discovers the list's purpose, he or she will be anxious to add to it.)

4. As your child reads related books, have him or her write book titles and write reviews under each subject on the list.

Reading Comprehension

Dear Parents,

Did You Know?

When you ask questions as your child reads a story, you help him or her better understand what was read. Asking questions also encourages your child to talk about his or her insights and ideas and explain his or her thoughts. Ask questions each time your child reads—you will learn about your child and he or she will learn from you.

How You Can Help

1. Before, during, and after your child reads, ask open-ended questions.

2. Before reading, ask questions such as:

   What do you think this story will be about? Why?
   What kind of book might this be—funny, sad, or something else? Why?

3. During reading, ask questions such as:

   What do you think will happen next?
   Why do you think that happened?

4. After reading, ask questions such as:

   What did you like most about the story?
   What did you like least?
   Which character interested you most? Why?
   Where did the story take place?
   Who was telling the story? How do you know?
   Was there anything in the story you didn't understand? If so, what?

Parent Letters for the Primary Grades ©1997 Creative Teaching Press

Dear Parents,

Did You Know?

When your child counts real objects, he or she learns what numbers actually mean. Younger children can easily understand the concept of 100 when they touch and gather 100 items. Older children begin to grasp the concepts of 1,000; 10,000; 100,000; and 1,000,000 when they make and count several groups of 100 objects. Try the following activity to help your child make numbers "count"!

How You Can Help

1. Before carving a pumpkin or watermelon, gather several small paper cups.

2. As you scoop out seeds, invite your child to count and place ten seeds (if your child is younger) or twenty seeds (if your child is older) in each cup.

3. After carving is complete, invite your child to count all the seeds by touching the cups and counting by tens or twenties.

4. Try the activity with other items such as cereal, M&Ms, or animal crackers.

Counting and Number Facts

Dear Parents,

Did You Know?

Skip counting—counting by twos, fives, tens, hundreds, odd numbers, or any other number pattern—helps your child in several ways. He or she learns that numbers follow a logical pattern, understands even and odd numbers, and becomes better at mental math (figuring out math problems in his or her head). Skip counting can be practiced by children of any age. Play the following game to help your child become a top-notch skip counter.

How You Can Help

1. To play *Buzz!,* choose a skip-count pattern such as fives.

2. Write the pattern on paper (for example, *5, 10, 15, 20, 25, 30, 35, 40, 45, 50).*

3. Take turns counting by ones—you say *one,* your child says *two,* and so on. When it's time to say *five,* substitute *buzz* for the word *five.*

4. Continue counting, but say *buzz* each time you reach one of the numbers in the pattern.

5. After reaching 50, have your child read the paper's skip-count pattern.

6. When your child is comfortable with one pattern, play with another such as multiples of three *(one, two, buzz, four, five, buzz, seven, eight, buzz . . .).*

Parent Letters for the Primary Grades ©1997 Creative Teaching Press

Dear Parents,

Did You Know?

Memorizing multiplication facts makes many math activities easier and faster to do. For example, when your child knows his or her math facts "by heart," he or she will be better at addition, division, and fractions. The following fun, easy game will give your child practice with multiplication and help make it "stick."

How You Can Help

1. Place a set of dominoes face down on a table and mix them up.

2. Draw five pieces, and have your child do the same.

3. To begin, have your child lay down any domino he or she chooses.

4. Lay down one of your dominoes so an end of yours and an end of your child's adds up to five, such as:

Or, lay down dominoes so ends have a product which is a multiple of five, such as: (Blank domino halves equal zero.)

5. If you cannot make five or a multiple of five, pick a domino from the pile until a play can be made. (You must keep all the dominoes you cannot use.)

6. Have your child take a turn and add a domino to make a sum or multiple of five.

7. Continue play until someone uses all of his or her dominoes. If all the dominoes are chosen and you and your child still have some left over, add the dots in each person's set. The person with the lowest dot total wins.

8. After you play with multiples of five, try multiples of other numbers such as three, four, and six.

Dear Parents,

Did You Know?

When your child knows multiplication number patterns, he or she has a better chance at math success. For example, 5 x 3 = 15 is another way to express the pattern *3 + 3 + 3 + 3 + 3 = 15* or *3, 6, 9, 12, 15*. When your child can look at multiplication in several ways, he or she will understand numbers follow logical, predictable patterns. Try the following multiplication pattern activity—even the youngest children can do it with your help!

How You Can Help

1. Complete this activity in two or three sessions.

2. Draw nine "hundreds charts" like that in the illustration (or reproduce the attached chart eight times).

3. Invite your child to circle multiples of two (2, 4, 6 . . .) on the first chart using a crayon or marker.

4. On the second chart, have your child circle multiples of three (3, 6, 9 . . .).

5. Continue using separate charts for your child to circle the multiples of four through ten.

6. Review each chart and have your child observe and describe its pattern, telling about beginning and ending numbers, odd and even numbers, and any special designs the circles made.

7. Lay out and review all the charts, comparing similarities and differences between them. (For example, the multiples of two and four consist of only even numbers.)

8. To close, have your child observe one chart and find "special numbers" such as odd numbers, numbers with the same two digits (11, 22, 33 . . .), numbers with digits that add up to eight (8, 17, 26 . . .), or numbers that have a four in the ones place (4, 14, 24 . . .).

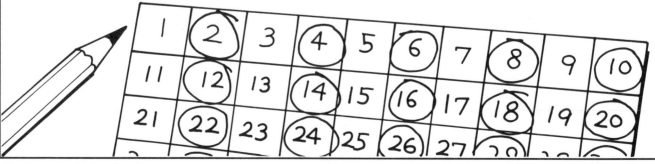

Parent Letters for the Primary Grades © 1997 Creative Teaching Press

Multiples Chart

1	2	3	4	5	6	7	8	9	10
11	12	13	14	15	16	17	18	19	20
21	22	23	24	25	26	27	28	29	30
31	32	33	34	35	36	37	38	39	40
41	42	43	44	45	46	47	48	49	50
51	52	53	54	55	56	57	58	59	60
61	62	63	64	65	66	67	68	69	70
71	72	73	74	75	76	77	78	79	80
81	82	83	84	85	86	87	88	89	90
91	92	93	94	95	96	97	98	99	100

Counting and Number Facts

Dear Parents,

Did You Know?

Mental math is math people do "in their heads," such as adding grocery totals and estimating cooking measurements. To do mental math, your child has to know his or her basic math facts "by heart." Try the following brainstretcher—your child gets practice with his or her basic facts and mental math because he or she has to *think* the answer instead of writing it.

How You Can Help

1. Help your child complete the addition problems on one of the attached charts.

2. Have your child read each problem aloud.

3. Invite him or her to cut the answer squares apart and place them in a container.

4. Have your child draw an answer square from the container. Ask him or her to "think out" each problem and place the square on the second chart. (If your child has difficulty, lay the square aside until all others have been placed.)

5. Time your child to see how fast he or she can complete the chart. Record the time.

6. Return all answer squares to the container and play another round. Have your child try to beat his or her first-round time.

7. When your child knows addition facts on the first chart, make a similar game using multiplication facts.

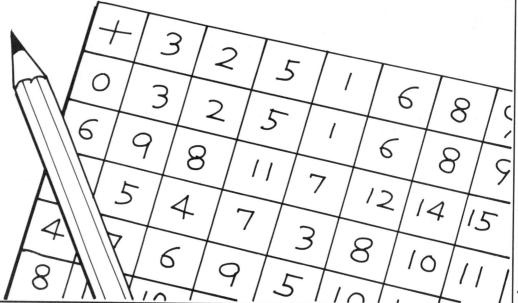

Parent Letters for the Primary Grades ©1997 Creative Teaching Press

Fill in the Facts

	3	2	5	1	6	8	9	7	4	0
0										
6										
2										
4										
8										
3										
7										
5										
1										
9										

Counting and Number Facts

Dear Parents,

Did You Know?

There are two kinds of subtraction—"take-away" subtraction, in which a smaller amount is taken away from a larger amount *(There were ten cookies. Sam ate three. How many were left?)* and "comparing" subtraction, in which numbers are compared *(There were five green birds and two red birds. How many more green birds were there than red birds?)*. To help your child with "comparing" subtraction, try the following activity.

How You Can Help

1. At first, play Luck of the Draw alone with your child. After your child learns the rules, he or she can play with a friend.

2. Remove face cards from a standard deck of playing cards. Place the rest of the deck face down.

3. Give yourself and your child an equal amount of counters such as toothpicks.

4. Draw a card and turn it over. Have your child do the same.

5. Recite a simple "comparing" story problem using the numbers shown, such as *I have five toothpicks. You have three. How many more toothpicks do I have than you?*

6. Using the counters, line up both sets of numbers, one set under the other. (The lineup will show how many more counters one has than the other.)

7. The person with the most counters tells the difference *(I have two more toothpicks than you.)* and takes that amount of counters from the other player (two).

8. Continue play until all the cards are used. The winner is the player with the most counters.

Parent Letters for the Primary Grades ©1997 Creative Teaching Press

Dear Parents,

Did You Know?

Estimation is important in math because it gives your child clues about an answer before he or she writes anything down. For example, if your child knows that 4 x 10 = 40, he or she knows the answer to 4 x 12 will be just a little more than 40. Use the following activity to help your child make "educated guesses" and improve his or her estimation skills.

How You Can Help

1. Hang an Estimation-of-the-Week question on your refrigerator door. Include questions such as *How many peanuts are in the jar? How many marshmallows are in the bag? How many pounds does this bag of groceries weigh? How many feet is it from one end of the living room to the other?*

2. Help your child think of ways to make "educated guesses" (estimations) about the questions, such as *Think about the number of peanuts in a small cup, and then guess how many cups would fit in the jar,* or *Count the amount of marshmallows on the outside wall of the bag, and then multiply that number by three or four.*

3. Invite your child and the rest of the family to secretly record their estimates. Read the estimates aloud when the family is together, count to find the actual answer, and congratulate the person who came closest.

4. To further sharpen your child's estimation skills, wonder out loud when you estimate, such as *I wonder how many pitchers of juice this can will make . . . .*

Dear Parents,

Did You Know?

Once your child becomes good at making number estimations (such as estimating the number of M&Ms in a glass), he or she can use the estimations to complete subtraction problems. Subtraction problems using estimation show your child that math has a purpose and is connected to real life. Try the following activity to help your child (and entire family) estimate and subtract.

How You Can Help

1. Each week, place several objects (oyster crackers, candy, or popcorn) in a large see-through container.

2. Place a "guessing box" next to the jar.

3. Display the jar and box for one week. Invite each family member to write his or her name on a paper slip and guess the amount of objects in the jar.

4. At the end of the week, have your child judge the estimations in the container by reading each family member's guess.

5. Invite your child to find the best guess and subtract that number from the group of objects. For example, if someone guessed 34 candies and there were really 48, your child would subtract 34 candies from the pile so 14 remained.

6. Have your child repeat the subtraction using the farthest-away guess.

Parent Letters for the Primary Grades ©1997 Creative Teaching Press

Dear Parents,

Did You Know?

Children love to measure because they get to touch and see math as well as write it. As your child learns measurement, he or she discovers we use the same units of measurement every time to make accurate measurements (standard measures). Help your child learn about standard measures by completing the following "handy" activity.

How You Can Help

1. Have your child trace his or her hand on heavy paper and cut it out.

2. Ask your child to choose several household objects such as a chair seat, a table-top, or a door. Ask him or her to estimate how many of his or her hands will go across each item.

3. Using the cutout as a measuring tool, show your child how to measure each item.

4. Trace and cut out your hand and complete the same activity. Have your child compare the results.

5. Show your child a ruler with inch or centimeter marks. Explain that everyone has to use either inches or centimeters to measure or, just like with two different hands, everyone would come up with different measurements.

One...

Estimation/Measurement

Dear Parents,

Did You Know?

When your child can logically go through steps to solve a real-life problem (such as learning to tie his or her shoes), he or she uses the same skills required to solve math problems. Try this "fruity" activity to help your child become a logical, problem-solving thinker.

How You Can Help

1. Ask your child, *Do all oranges have the same number of sections? the same number of seeds? the same size seeds? Are big seeds found in big oranges and little seeds in little oranges? How can we find out?*

2. Have your child brainstorm ways to answer your questions. If your child needs help with ideas, have him or her collect several types of oranges, pry them open (sections intact), and observe and count their sections and seeds. (All same-type oranges should have the same number of sections, but seed counts will vary.)

3. Have your child record his or her results on a graph, as shown.

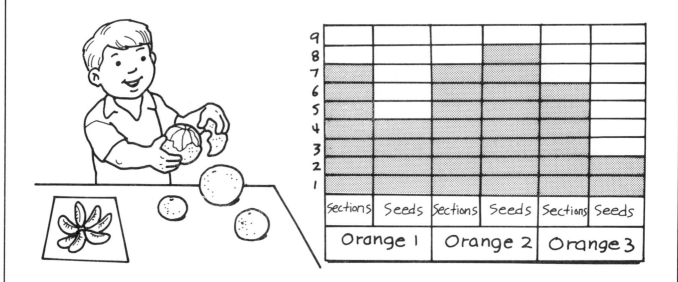

Parent Letters for the Primary Grades ©1997 Creative Teaching Press

Dear Parents,

Did You Know?

A skillful problem-solver knows how to think ahead and make a successful plan. Competitive games such as checkers, chess, or backgammon often involve mathematical problem-solving skills. Teach your child to play Reaching 20 to sharpen his or her game-playing and problem-solving skills.

How You Can Help

1. Take turns counting one or two numbers aloud until someone reaches 20.

2. The first player can say *one* or *one, two*. The second player then says the next number, *two* or *three* or the next two numbers, *two, three* or *three, four*.

3. The player to say *20* is the winner.

4. After the first round, explain that the game asks players to think ahead and plan what he or she should do based on what the other player does. Tell your child that thinking ahead and planning is important when he or she does things such as shopping, cooking, woodworking, art projects, gardening, sewing, or car repair.

5. Play two or three more rounds until your child sharpens his or her strategic skills.

Problem Solving

Dear Parents,

Did You Know?

A terrific way to help your child learn his or her math facts and develop essential problem-solving skills is to play games and solve puzzles. Children can easily learn complex math and problem-solving skills when excited and having fun. Improve your child's skills by playing Which Side of the Tracks?—he or she will soon be "chugging along"!

How You Can Help

1. Invite your child to write the number *one* above or below the track.

2. Tell your child he or she will write numbers above or below the track in counting order, but it is against the rules to have three numbers that make an addition problem on the same side. For example, two, three, and five cannot be on the same side because 2 + 3 = 5.

3. Invite your child to place the two above or below the track.

4. When your child places the three, remind him or her not to put it on the same side as one and two if they are on the same side of the track. However, if the one and two are on different sides, the three can be written on either.

5. If your child is not able to place a given number on either side, have him or her draw a new track and start over. In a short time, your child will be able to plan ahead and reach six.

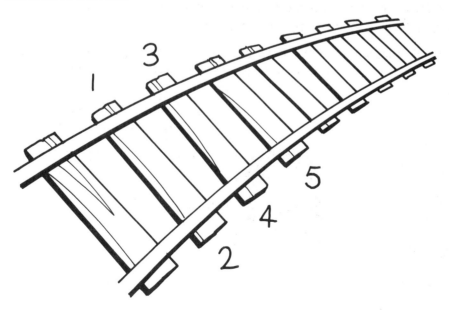

Parent Letters for the Primary Grades ©1997 Creative Teaching Press

Dear Parents,

Did You Know?

People use math in their everyday lives because solving math problems solves real-life problems. For example, people solve math problems when they decide what to wear based on the outside temperature. Try the following problem-solving activity to help your child see the connection between math and real life—it's "hot"!

How You Can Help

1. During the change of seasons, place a thermometer outside early in the morning.

2. Have your child step outside and feel the temperature, deciding what to wear based on how it feels.

3. Have your child read and record the temperature on the thermometer.

4. The next morning, have your child stay inside. Go outside and read and record the temperature. Bring in your results.

5. Read both days' results to your child. Ask him or her to compare that day's temperature to the previous day's. Have him or her remember how the temperature felt the previous morning and think about the previous day's temperature number compared to the present day's number.

6. Based on numbers only, have your child decide if he or she needs short sleeves, a sweatshirt, or a coat. Help your child by asking questions such as *Look at today's and yesterday's temperatures. Is today's number higher or lower than yesterday's? Remember, the higher the number, the warmer the weather.*

7. Tell your child that since he or she could relate how a temperature felt to a number, he or she was able to read a temperature and solve a problem.

Problem Solving /Temperature

Dear Parents,

Did You Know?

Word problems ask a lot of your child. First, he or she has to read and understand the words that make up the problem. Next, your child has to decide if he or she should add, subtract, multiply, divide, or do a combination of operations. Finally, when these steps are complete, your child can write numbers and find an answer. To make these steps easier, try the following activity.

How You Can Help

1. Write a simple word problem such as *Farmer Fred had seven pigs. Three pigs got out and ran away. How many pigs were left on the farm?*

2. Tell your child the first step in a word problem is to read it carefully several times. Have your child read the problem at least three times. Help him or her read any new words.

3. Tell your child the next step is to decide if he or she should add, subtract, multiply, or divide. Explain that whenever a problem asks a person to "take away" things and find leftovers, the problem is asking him or her to subtract.

4. Explain that one way to solve a subtraction problem is to draw a picture of it. Ask your child to draw seven pigs inside a farm fence.

5. Have your child say the number of pigs that ran away (three), erase them, and draw them running away on the other side of the fence.

6. Ask your child to read the question at the end of the word problem. Ask him or her to count the number of pigs left on the farm (four).

7. Repeat the activity with an addition, multiplication, and division problem.

Parent Letters for the Primary Grades ©1997 Creative Teaching Press

Dear Parents,

Did You Know?

Word problems are easier for children when they visualize the situations as if they are really happening and use real objects to represent those in the problems. When you show your child how to connect math to real life, you help him or her solve word problems and become a better all-around math student.

How You Can Help

1. Begin word-problem practice with real-life situations. For example, when your child is setting the table, say, *There are four plates on the table. You're going to put down two more. How many plates will there be when you are done?*

2. Invite your child to touch the plates, count them, and get the total. Then, ask your child what he or she did to get the answer (add).

3. When your child can do real word problems, make up problems and have him or her use counters such as beans to represent numbers.

4. For example, tell the story, *One day, a boy ran three miles at track practice. The next practice, he ran seven miles. How many fewer miles did the boy run the first time?* Have your child set out three counters on one side of the table and seven counters on the other side. Ask your child to make matches by taking away pairs of counters (one from each side) until no counters are left on one side. Have your child count and tell the number of leftover counters (four) and explain what he or she did to get the answer (subtract). Explain that when a problem asks you to compare things and find out how many more or fewer there are, the problem uses subtraction.

5. When making up problems, mix addition, subtraction, multiplication, and division so your child gets a variety of practice.

There will be six plates.

Problem Solving

Dear Parents,

Did You Know?

When your child understands that the four in 14 means a lot less than the four in 40 or 400, he or she is on the way to understanding place value. To help your child learn that a number written in a different place has a different meaning, play Roll for 100. Your child will soon learn the value of numbers in the tens and ones places, not to mention have a great time!

How You Can Help

1. Make a score sheet for you and your child, as shown.

2. Using tape, cover the four, five, and six on a die.

3. Take turns rolling the die with your child until you each roll five numbers.

4. After each roll, you and your child write the number rolled in either the *tens* or *ones* column on the score sheet. If you or your child write the number in the *tens* column, write a zero in the *ones* column to complete the number.

5. As you play, show your child how to plan a strategy each time the die is rolled so his or her final total will be close to 100.

6. After you have each rolled five numbers, total the numbers written. The winner is the player whose total is closest to 100 without going over.

Parent Letters for the Primary Grades ©1997 Creative Teaching Press

Dear Parents,

Did You Know?

Each year, your child learns about numbers with higher and higher place value, from ones all the way to trillions. When your child reaches upper-elementary grades, he or she will learn about values lower than one through the study of decimals. To help your child review place value, play a new version of the game *20 Questions*. Your child will never suspect he or she is learning!

How You Can Help

1. To begin, choose a range of numbers, such as one to 25 or (for an older child) one to one million. Tell your child the range.

2. Keeping it to yourself, pick one number within the range. Your child's job is to identify the number by asking "yes-or-no" questions.

3. Have your child ask questions such as *Is the number higher than __? Is the number in the hundreds? tens? ones? Is it an odd number? an even number?* Encourage your child to ask broad questions instead of guessing numbers randomly.

4. Help your child learn strategies that eliminate several numbers with one question. For example, if the range is one to 50, your child could eliminate half the numbers by asking, *Is the number higher than 25?* Using the answer as a clue, your child can quickly narrow the range.

5. After each clue, chat about what is now known about the number and how this can help your child think of what to ask next.

6. When your child guesses the number, trade roles, and invite your child to think of a number.

Place Value

Dear Parents,

Did You Know?

Learning about money is a life skill that helps your child with all kinds of math such as place value. A great way to begin teaching money skills is to have your child count money and make combinations for the same value. Try the following "on-the-money" activity to help your child increase his or her money skills.

How You Can Help

1. Complete this activity in two sessions. Collect loose change or purchase play money.

2. Make a different chart (see attached) for a nickel, dime, quarter, 50-cent piece, and dollar.

3. To begin, display a nickel. Have your child pull coins toward him or her that together equal a nickel (five pennies is the only combination). Write *5* under *pennies* on your child's chart and have him or her read the answer to you.

4. Then, have your child pull coins to make combinations that equal a dime (ten pennies, one nickel and five pennies, and two nickels). Record his or her answers on the chart.

5. After nickels and dimes, have your child work with quarters. Since there are several combinations for quarters, end the first session after charting quarter combinations.

6. To begin the second session, have your child review by pulling down nickel, dime, and quarter combinations (with no chart recording).

7. Then, have your child pull down combinations for the 50-cent piece. Record his or her answers on the chart. (There are 49 fifty-cent-piece combinations!)

8. Close the activity with a dollar. (There are 251 combinations for a dollar!)

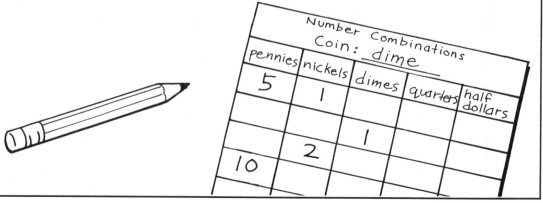

Parent Letters for the Primary Grades ©1997 Creative Teaching Press

Number Combinations

Coin: _____

pennies	nickels	dimes	quarters	half dollars

Money

Dear Parents,

Did You Know?

Making change is one of the most difficult money skills for children to master because it requires them to subtract "in their heads." Luckily, there is a fun way to teach your child to make and receive the correct change. Help your child make a toy store, and watch his or her imagination and money skills grow!

How You Can Help

1. Using stickers as price tags, help your child write a price for as many toys as he or she wishes. Be sure prices are under one dollar.

2. On a bed, set up a "cash register" with real or play money.

3. Pretend to be the store clerk. (This is creative-play time—really "ham it up.") Give your child one dollar to spend. Tell him or her to shop for one toy and bring it to the cash register when he or she is ready to "check out."

4. Ask him or her for the money and show how to count out the change for the dollar he or she gave you.

5. Trade places. Shop for a toy and help your child make change for you.

6. Play toy store several times with one toy until your child is comfortable making change.

7. To make the activity more challenging, play with five dollars (more difficult changing skills) or have the shopper choose two or more toys totaling no more than a dollar (mental addition skills).

Parent Letters for the Primary Grades © 1997 Creative Teaching Press

Dear Parents,

Did You Know?

Kids love fractions when they can eat food while learning them! Pizzas and pies are naturals for teaching eighths, graham crackers help with fourths, and sandwiches are perfect for teaching halves and fourths. Help your child develop a taste for fractions with the following fraction activity.

How You Can Help

1. Make two peanut butter and jelly sandwiches—one for you and one for your child.

2. Help your child cut his or her sandwich into two equal parts. Explain that the two parts are equal and each piece is called a *half*. Write *1/2* on a napkin.

3. Count the pieces (*one-half, two-halves*) aloud. Write *2/2* (two-halves).

4. Cut your sandwich into four equal parts, explaining that each is the same size. Tell your child that each part is called a *fourth* because the sandwich has been divided into four equal parts. Write *1/4*.

5. Count *one-fourth, two-fourths, three-fourths, four-fourths.* Write *1/4, 2/4, 3/4,* and *4/4.*

6. Have your child position two of your fourths on top of one of his or her halves. Ask, *Is your sandwich piece the same size as mine? Could we say that one-half is equal to two-fourths?*

7. Lay one whole sandwich on top of the other. Ask, *Is four-fourths equal to two-halves?* Help your child cut his or her sandwich into fourths.

8. Have your child eat two of his or her pieces. Eat one of yours. Help your child figure out that he or she has two-fourths left and you have three-fourths.

9. Invite your child to count the remaining pieces to get five-fourths. Ask, *How many whole sandwiches could you make from five-fourths?* Have your child piece the parts together to show that five-fourths equal one whole sandwich plus one-fourth.

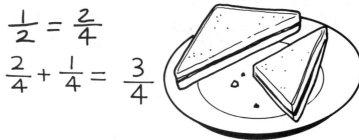

$$\frac{1}{2} = \frac{2}{4}$$

$$\frac{2}{4} + \frac{1}{4} = \frac{3}{4}$$

Dear Parents,

Did You Know?

Fractions can be confusing because higher numbers in the bottom parts of fractions stand for smaller pieces. For example, one-eighth (1/8) of a cherry pie is smaller than one-fourth (1/4). To help your child understand that a bigger bottom number means a smaller piece in "fraction language," make fraction snowflakes.

How You Can Help

1. Give your child three coffee filters and a pair of scissors.

2. Have your child fold the first filter in half, and then cut geometric shapes along the edge and in the middle. Have him or her open the filter, displaying a snowflake design. Write *1/2* with felt-tip marker on each side of the fold, and say, *one-half, two-halves.*

3. Have your child fold the second filter into fourths, make a snowflake, and open it up. Write *1/4* on each section, and say, *one-fourth, two-fourths, three-fourths, four-fourths.*

4. Repeat the activity with the third filter, folding it into eighths.

5. Cut one section from each snowflake. Have your child place the sections in order from smallest to largest.

6. Ask your child to read the bottom number in each fraction aloud. Explain that in fractions, when top numbers are the same and bottom numbers are higher, the piece with the highest number is smallest.

Parent Letters for the Primary Grades ©1997 Creative Teaching Press

Dear Parents,

Did You Know?

Spatial reasoning, the ability to figure out how something goes together and comes apart, is an important math skill. Puzzles are an excellent introduction to spatial reasoning. As your child works to fit pieces, he or she learns about shapes and how they go together. Make and use puzzles, and watch your child's spatial-reasoning skills soar!

How You Can Help

1. Cut a picture from a magazine. Paste it onto a thin sheet of cardboard. The picture serves as the back of the puzzle (the answer key). Your child should not look at the picture unless he or she needs help.

2. Turn the picture over. Make one cut in a straight, diagonal line. Be sure the cut goes from one edge of the puzzle to the other edge, not through corners. (If corners are cut, the puzzle becomes too difficult.)

3. Invite your child to put the two-piece puzzle together, looking at the top (cardboard) side only.

4. Cut the puzzle one more time to make three pieces and have your child put it together. When your child needs help, have him or her turn the pieces over and use the picture as a guide.

5. As an extra challenge, cut the puzzle again and have your child put together four pieces. (Refer to the diagram to see one way to cut a four-piece puzzle.)

6. When your child can complete the first puzzle quickly, use new pictures and challenge him or her to complete other three- and four-piece puzzles.

Dear Parents,

Did You Know?

Even if your child can quickly give an answer when adding two numbers, he or she may need extra time to think of the two numbers when given the answer first. For example, asking your child for two numbers that add up to 15 may take longer to answer than if you asked, *What is eight plus seven?* To help your child think of addition "frontward" and backward, play Sum It Up. It'll really get him or her thinking!

How You Can Help

1. Make two game sheets by writing numbers one through twelve across two sheets of paper. Give one sheet to your child and keep one for yourself.

2. Go first by rolling a pair of dice. Cross out either the sum of the dice or any two numbers that add up to the sum. For example, if you roll a five and two, you can cross out the seven (5 + 2 = 7) or any pair of numbers other than five and two that equal seven.

3. Invite your child to take a turn.

4. During a turn, if a player cannot cross out numbers (because they are already crossed out), he or she has to pass the dice to the other player. The first person to cross out all his or her numbers is the winner.

5. After you and your child can play easily with two dice, try playing with three (writing numbers to 18) or four (writing numbers to 24).

Parent Letters for the Primary Grades © 1997 Creative Teaching Press

Dear Parents,

Did You Know?

As adults, we do math "in our heads" every day—we add, subtract, measure, estimate, and do other math-related activities. Although it seems to come naturally, doing math in our heads is not automatic. It takes practice, and that's what children need. Help your child practice mental math by playing a Japanese card game called Kabu.

How You Can Help

1. Remove all face cards from a deck of playing cards. Deal two cards to yourself and two to your child. In your head, add your cards and have your child do the same.

2. The object of the game is to get your cards to add up to nine or as close to nine as possible. (To do this, you or your child can draw a third or fourth card.)

3. Here's the trick—if your cards total ten or more, only the number in the ones place counts. For example, if you have a three, three, and seven, your total is 13, but only the three counts toward your score (because 13 is more than ten). Since your playing total is three, you could choose another card. If you chose a six, you would have a "perfect nine." But if you chose a seven, your total would be ten and your score would be zero! You would then keep choosing (up to a fourth card) until you got as close to nine as possible.

4. After each player draws up to four cards, add the totals and record them.

5. Keep a running score. The first player who comes closest to 48 without going over is the winner.

Dear Parents,

Did You Know?

Your child learns valuable math skills each time he or she plays a game. With a board game, your child learns counting skills as he or she moves a marker. Card games teach your child patterns, counting, and addition skills. With checkers or chess, your child learns problem-solving and logic skills. Play games such as the following with your child—he or she will experience a lot more than a good time!

How You Can Help

1. Set 13 counters (12 of one type, one of another) in a line. Use counters such as coins, buttons, or checkers. The last counter is called *Poison.*

2. Take turns removing one or two counters at a time.

3. The player who takes Poison is the loser.

4. Play the game several times until your child can anticipate your moves and find a sure way to win.

Parent Letters for the Primary Grades © 1997 Creative Teaching Press

Dear Parents,

Did You Know?

When your child plays individual number games such as solitaire, he or she is learning problem solving. Problem solving helps your child in every subject area—it gives him or her the extra push needed to finish challenging work. Start your child on the problem-solving track by teaching him or her to play Pyramid Power.

How You Can Help

1. Using the attached number pyramid, place a marker such as a penny over each circle, except for circle one.

2. Have your child play the game by jumping one marker over another to land on an empty circle. When jumping a marker, have your child remove it from the game board and keep it.

3. To begin, have your child move the marker from circle four to circle one or the marker from circle six to circle one. Explain that he or she can only jump markers attached by a diagonal or horizontal line.

4. Have your child make jumps until he or she has no other jumps left.

5. Ask your child to count the number of markers left on the board.

6. Challenge your child to play until he or she can remove more and more markers with each game. Your child is the "puzzle master" when he or she can remove all markers but one.

Pyramid Power

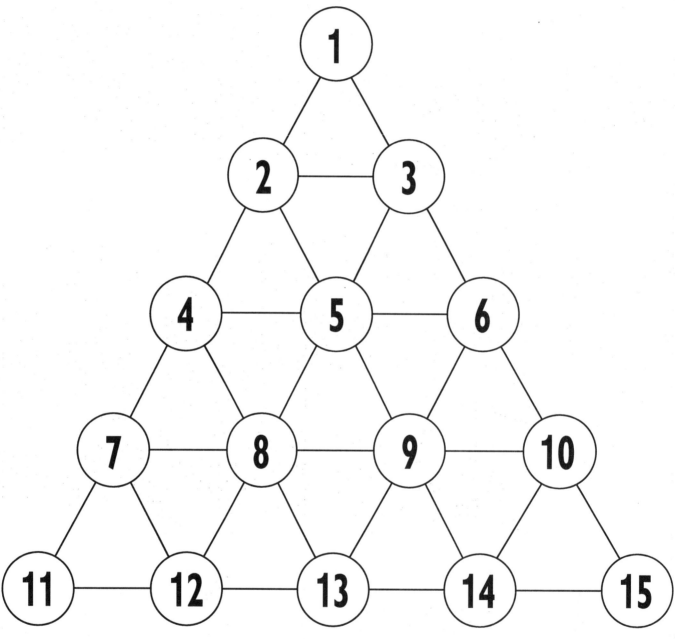

Parent Letters for the Primary Grades ©1997 Creative Teaching Press

Dear Parents,

Did You Know?

Mentally adding numbers is an important math (and life) skill. Games such as darts and bowling take the work out of math and help your child add numbers mentally. Try another mental math game called One Hundred to help your child add "in his or her head."

How You Can Help

1. Give one of the attached game boards to your child and keep one for yourself.

2. Place a marker at the bottom of both columns on each board.

3. Roll two dice and mentally add the total. Move your marker to show the number you rolled. If the sum is more than nine, use both markers and move up the tens and ones columns.

4. Have your child take a turn. If your child needs help adding the score, have him or her write it out. Offer help when needed.

5. Take turns rolling the dice, adding numbers to the previous score, and moving up the columns.

6. The first player to reach 100 is the winner.

One Hundred

100
90
80
70
60
50
40
30
20
10
Place Marker Here

9
8
7
6
5
4
3
2
1
Place Marker Here

Parent Letters for the Primary Grades ©1997 Creative Teaching Press

Dear Parents,

Did You Know?

Of all language-arts skills (speaking, reading, listening, and writing), we develop listening and speaking first. As your child develops as a speaker and listener, he or she becomes a better reader and writer as well. To develop your child's speaking skills, hold a Family News Hour—your child will learn about language as well as your family!

How You Can Help

1. Once a week, have a Family News Hour in which each family member describes a recent experience, demonstrates a new skill, talks about a new possession, discusses a book, or shares any other information. Have adults and older children speak first to model for younger children.

2. To make Family News Hour extra fun for younger children, provide them with props. Have younger children stand behind an appliance box with a cutout square so it looks like they are "on TV." Invite them to use a microphone from a tape recorder and become a news reporter.

3. Vary Family News Hour by having a family member be an "anchor person" and introduce or interview speakers.

4. If your child wishes, help him or her write a presentation to read at Family News Hour.

Speaking and Listening

Dear Parents,

Did You Know?

As your child develops, he or she learns how to sort items into categories—a skill known as classification. Young children can sort items into broad categories, such as sorting animals from furniture. Older children can take sorting a step further and sort items into narrow categories, such as sorting animals into specific groups—farm animals, forest animals, and pets. Help your child learn about categories by playing Long Lists.

How You Can Help

1. Explain the word *category*—a group of ideas, things, or words that have something in common.

2. Pick a category such as football teams, rough things, or desserts.

3. Take turns with your child naming words that fit into the category. For example, for rough things you might say, *tree bark, rocks,* or *sandpaper.*

4. Create the longest list possible. Do not write the words, but mentally keep track of the number of items listed. Write the number on scrap paper under the category's name.

5. Choose a new category and play again. Write the second name and record the number of items listed.

6. Continue play with a third category. With each round of play, try to beat your previous score.

Parent Letters for the Primary Grades ©1997 Creative Teaching Press

Dear Parents,

Did You Know?

When you encourage your child to play with words by inventing and saying sentences, you help him or her develop a larger vocabulary and become a better speaker, listener, reader, and writer. Play Saying Silly Sentences with your child—once you see how fun and easy it is, you and your child will quickly create sentence activities on your own!

How You Can Help

1. Find old greeting cards, magazines, postcards, coloring books, catalogs, or calendars with pictures that show only one item.

2. Cut out the pictures and mount them on large index cards. Label each card with the picture's name.

3. Shuffle the cards and place them in a pile, picture-side down.

4. Draw the top three cards and turn them face up.

5. Try to make up and say a complete sentence using the three words. If you are successful, keep the cards. If not, invite your child to try.

6. If neither you nor your child can make a sentence, put the cards in a discard pile to be reshuffled when the original pile is gone.

7. Have your child take a turn drawing cards and making up sentences. Take turns until all cards are gone.

Parent Letters for the Primary Grades ©1997 Creative Teaching Press

Dear Parents,

Did You Know?

Everyone loves to talk about their own experiences. When you invite your child to speak about his or her life, you help him or her in several ways—you increase your child's self-esteem, develop his or her vocabulary, and show him or her that stories have a beginning, middle, and end. Invite your child to share his or her life stories by making and sharing Story Scrolls.

How You Can Help

1. Help your child think of an exciting event he or she experienced, such as a trip, sporting event, birthday, or holiday.

2. Help your child break the event into parts by telling what happened first, second, third, fourth, and last.

3. Invite your child to illustrate each story part on a separate piece of paper.

4. Place the pictures side-by-side in order. Tape the pictures' sides together.

5. Tape the edge of the first picture to an empty paper towel or wrapping paper roll. Tape the last picture to the end of a second tube.

6. Starting with the last picture, roll the pictures right to left onto the second tube. (The first tube serves as a handle.)

7. Gather the family. Invite your child to narrate as he or she unrolls the scroll and tells his or her story as the pictures are revealed.

Parent Letters for the Primary Grades ©1997 Creative Teaching Press

Dear Parents,

Did You Know?

Encouraging your child to make up and tell stories helps him or her think creatively, develop speaking skills, and understand the link between speaking and listening. Turn your child into a first-class storyteller by playing the following imagination game. You can play it any time or anywhere—in a car, a waiting room, at home, or any place you and your child can talk together.

How You Can Help

1. Think of a sentence that begins a story, such as *One bright, sunny morning, Cooper and Tana went out to play in the park.* Be sure to include two characters and the setting in the first sentence.

2. Invite your child to think of and say a sentence to add to the story. For example, your child might add, *Cooper and Tana were on the slide when they looked down and saw a little purple man running under it.*

3. Take turns adding sentences to the story until it comes to a natural ending.

Speaking and Listening

Dear Parents,

Did You Know?

Even when your child can read, you can use wordless books to help him or her develop speaking, reading, and writing skills. Wordless books offer a complete story just waiting to be told by your child. Try the following wordless-book activity to see how easy it is to develop your child's skills.

How You Can Help

1. Invite your child to look through each page of a wordless book and invent a story in his or her mind. Encourage your child to think of names for the characters and places in the story.

2. Have your child "read" the story to you, flipping to each page as he or she speaks.

3. After your child has told the story, ask him or her questions about it, such as *What was the problem in the story? How did the problem get solved?*

4. To extend learning, have your child "read" the story again. (Don't worry if the words change.) Write his or her words on sticky notes and place them on the correct book pages.

5. Read the sticky notes back to your child.

6. Keep the notes in place so your child can read his or her own story again and again.

Parent Letters for the Primary Grades ©1997 Creative Teaching Press

Dear Parents,

Did You Know?

Children love to get mail, and one sure way they can get it is to write and send letters. Letter writing helps your child learn how to put ideas on paper, spell, and use correct grammar. To make writing letters extra special, invite your child to make his or her own stationery. The activity below describes how.

How You Can Help

1. Show your child several stationery samples such as those you receive in the mail, company letterhead, or personal stationery.

2. Ask your child to brainstorm some advantages of having personal stationery (such as the reader immediately knows who the writer is or the reader has a way to remember who wrote him or her).

3. Provide your child with paper and art supplies with which to design personal stationery.

4. Encourage your child to create more than one design by adding leaf, fingerprint, flower, or initial borders.

5. Have your child top the stationery with his or her name or a self portrait.

6. When your child completes the designs, make photocopies (color, if possible) so he or she has a large supply.

7. Help your child list people and organizations to write, such as relatives, toy companies, or favorite movie stars.

8. Once a month, have your child use his or her stationery and write a letter to someone on the list. Soon your child will be getting replies!

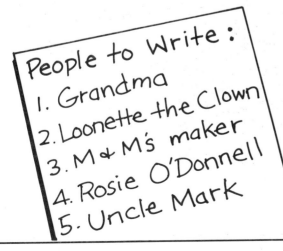

Dear Parents,

Did You Know?

Sometimes parents hear, *I can't think of what to write!* from their developing writers. If you hear this from your child, he or she needs ideas. Luckily, there are several ways to help your child with ideas—you can have him or her read a book and get ideas from the plot, generate ideas from a personal experience, or play games to think of characters, settings, and plots. Paper-Bag Writer is one game that will help your child think of writing ideas.

How You Can Help

1. Gather three small paper bags. Label one bag *characters,* one *settings,* and one *actions*.

2. Help your child brainstorm ten story characters (such as an astronaut), ten settings (such as a haunted house), and ten actions (such as finding a locked chest).

3. Write each item on a paper strip. Place the paper strips in the appropriate bags.

4. When it's story-writing time, invite your child to pick one piece of paper from each bag and create a story using those three elements.

5. Depending on your child's writing level, he or she can dictate the story to you while you write it, tell it through drawing cartoons and writing short captions, or write it him- or herself.

Parent Letters for the Primary Grades ©1997 Creative Teaching Press

Dear Parents,

Did You Know?

When writing is seen as enjoyable rather than a chore, your child will choose to write in his or her free time. Three of the best ways to encourage your child to write are to write yourself (in front of your child), create a pleasing writing environment, and provide opportunities for writing. Use Getting Them to Write to accomplish these goals. Your child's attitude toward writing (and his or her report card) will greatly benefit!

How You Can Help

1. Provide a special place for writing. Be sure the place is in a quiet area with a comfortable chair, a table or desk, and good lighting.

2. In the writing area, provide a wide variety of writing supplies such as pens; pencils; crayons; markers; paints; chalk and chalkboard; and lined, scrap, or colored paper. Provide envelopes and postage stamps as well.

3. Encourage your child to write any and all the time, but set aside a special writing time each week. Writing time can include short sessions such as having your child create a shopping list or longer sessions such as having your child write a story or a new ending for a just-read book.

4. For an everyday activity, hang a large piece of posterboard in a high-traffic area to create a Family Billboard. Invite family members to write messages, jokes, reminders, and questions whenever they wish. Read the billboard with your child and change the posterboard as it fills.

Parent Letters for the Primary Grades ©1997 Creative Teaching Press

Dear Parents,

Did You Know?

Your child may be surprised to learn that poems do not have to rhyme. Haiku is one example of poetry without rhyme. Help your child experience non-rhyming poetry by writing Haiku. Haiku poems are short, easy, and fun!

How You Can Help

1. Help your child pick the poem's subject by choosing an object in nature, such as a tree, butterfly, horse, or raindrop.

2. Haiku poems have three lines. For line one, have your child think of a phrase about the subject that has five syllables, such as *The wind is blowing*.

3. To check the syllable count, have your child clap each syllable as he or she says the words aloud.

4. For line two, ask your child to think of a phrase that has seven syllables, such as *Whispering, gently blowing*.

5. For line three, have your child think of another five-syllable phrase to end the poem, such as *Soft wind in my hair*.

6. Invite your child to write the poem on drawing paper and read it to you.

7. Have your child illustrate the poem. Display it in a prominent place for everyone to read and admire.

The wind is blowing.
Whispering, gently blowing.
Soft wind in my hair.

Parent Letters for the Primary Grades ©1997 Creative Teaching Press

Dear Parents,

Did You Know?

Your child will learn at least four types of writing in school—narrative (story writing), expository (telling facts), descriptive (describing ideas, objects, and situations), and persuasive (convincing others). A fun way to help your child get some persuasive-writing practice is to have him or her write to convince you to buy a gift. With a purpose like that, any child will gladly write!

How You Can Help

1. Invite your child to name one gift (that you can afford) he or she would like to receive for a holiday, birthday, or any occasion.

2. Tell your child that to receive the gift, he or she must convince you, in writing, to buy it.

3. Explain that this kind of writing is called persuasive writing because the writer is trying to persuade the reader to do something.

4. Depending on your child's ability level, have him or her dictate as you write or write it him- or herself.

5. Have your child begin the paragraph by stating (in a complete sentence) what he or she wants.

6. In the paragraph's body, have your child give at least three reasons why he or she should have the item. Have your child add to the paragraph by writing ideas that will convince you to buy the gift, such as promising to do (or not do) something if he or she receives it.

7. Have your child close the paragraph by politely asking for the gift.

8. Ask your child to read the paragraph to you and then, as a reward, shop!

I need new tennis shoes because my old ones have holes.

Parent Letters for the Primary Grades ©1997 Creative Teaching Press

Writing

Dear Parents,

Did You Know?

Descriptive writing asks your child to use words that express ideas in a clear, thorough way. Throughout school, your child will use descriptive writing when he or she writes about science experiments, historical events, objects, or personal experiences. Help your child practice descriptive writing with the following activity. After trying it once, your child will be "hungry" for more!

How You Can Help

1. Prepare a family-sized portion of food new to your child, such as a pomegranate, peanut brittle, or kale. Hide the food.

2. Blindfold your child, and have him or her taste the food before hiding it again.

3. Have your child say five sentences describing the food's taste. Write his or her description on paper.

4. Show the food to your child. Have him or her write five sentences describing the food's appearance.

5. Tell the name of the food and any facts you know about it, such as where it's from and whether it is a fruit, vegetable, meat, grain, or a combination.

6. Gather the family at the dinner table for a guessing game. Have your child read his or her sentences to the family. Invite family members to guess the food.

7. Then, reveal the food's name, and serve it for everyone to enjoy.

It tastes like there are peanuts in it.

Parent Letters for the Primary Grades © 1997 Creative Teaching Press

Dear Parents,

Did You Know?

Sometimes it's easier for a child to play games to learn spelling rather than rely on rote memorization. Play a variation of Scrabble to help your child practice spelling and word-building skills. You don't need a purchased game—a homemade version is explained below!

How You Can Help

1. Cut out at least 50 small paper squares. On each, have your child write a letter of the alphabet. (The letter Q should be paired with U. Make duplicates of vowels and common consonants such as M, N, S, T, R, and L.)

2. Decide in advance whether to allow proper nouns (those that begin with capital letters, such as *Louise* or *Boston*.)

3. Place the letters in a small paper bag and shake it to mix them up. Pull six letters from the bag.

4. With these letters, you have three minutes to make as many words as possible. (For example, a pick of E, B, N, D, O, and S could lead to the words *bend, bond, bonds, bone, bones, done, son, do, doe, does, so, snob, bed, beds, be, end, ends, send, sob,* and *sod*).

5. Write down each word after you make it.

6. After your turn, return the letters to the bag for your child's turn. Help him or her make words, if needed.

7. Take turns and play three or four rounds. The winner is the player who builds the most words.

Parent Letters for the Primary Grades ©1997 Creative Teaching Press

Spelling

Dear Parents,

Did You Know?

Your child will remember words that are important to him or her. For example, your child is more likely to correctly spell words he or she speaks, reads, and writes every day. A great way to help your child remember how to spell his or her own favorite words is to create a personal dictionary. Help your child make his or her own dictionary by trying the following activity.

How You Can Help

1. Have your child choose a special interest or hobby as the subject of his or her dictionary, such as basketball, model building, dancing, or sewing.

2. Invite your child to use art supplies (such as paint pens, puffy paint, felt, sequins, and glue) to decorate the cover of a three-ring binder.

3. Place 26 pieces of loose-leaf notebook paper in the binder. Have your child label each page with a letter of the alphabet.

4. The first time your child uses his or her dictionary, ask him or her to think of five words related to the chosen interest or hobby.

5. Help your child write each word on its corresponding notebook page, write a definition next to the word, and illustrate an example of it.

6. Each time your child finishes an interest or hobby for the day, invite him or her to add new words to the dictionary.

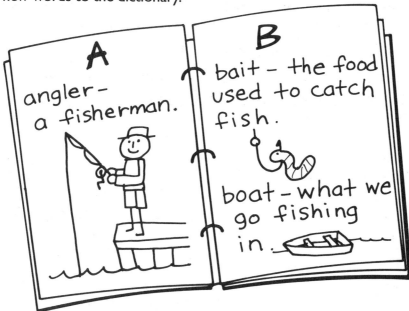

Parent Letters for the Primary Grades ©1997 Creative Teaching Press

Dear Parents,

Did You Know?

When your child becomes comfortable building and manipulating letters and words, he or she becomes a better speller, reader, and writer. Word puzzles and games such as the following improve letter and word skills while inviting your child to have fun. Play Four by Four with your child—soon he or she will have the "write" stuff!

How You Can Help

1. Cut out 36 equal-sized paper squares. Write a letter of the alphabet on each square, writing Q and U together for the letter Q. On the extra squares, make two additional vowel sets (A, E, I, O, U).

2. Draw two blank four-by-four grids, one for you and one for your child. Determine a point value such as 50 to win.

3. To play, lay out all the letters face down and mix them up. Pick a single letter and call it out.

4. You and your child write the letter in any square on your grids.

5. Then invite your child to pick a letter to call out. Again, write the letter in your grids.

6. The goal is to build words of two or more letters in "crossword style" —across or down. Words can take up fewer than four squares. Empty spaces can be filled with letters that don't spell words. (See the illustration for an example.) After letters are written, they cannot be moved to other spaces.

7. Take turns pulling letters until all spaces are filled.

8. Total your points—two-letter words earn two points, three-letter words earn three, and four-letter words earn four. The first player to reach the agreed-upon point level wins.

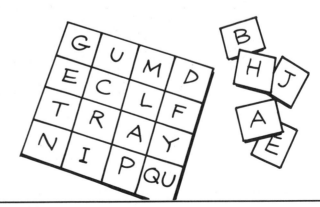

```
ACROSS:    GUM = 3
           TRAY= 4
           RAY = 3
           NIP = 3
DOWN:      GET = 3
           LAP = 3
        Total = 19
```

Spelling

Dear Parents,

Did You Know?

To get the most from crossword puzzles, have your child use them "the other way around" by making up a crossword puzzle for others to solve. Making up clues helps your child think of different ways to say the same thing, developing his or her vocabulary and self-esteem as he or she challenges family members to complete the puzzle.

How You Can Help

1. Have your child choose several spelling words. Show your child how to fill in the words on an empty grid, making words connect across and down by sharing letters.

2. Have your child color in squares that do not contain letters.

3. Add a number to the first letter of each word to show which clue references that word.

4. On a separate paper, help your child write clues for the puzzle answers. Clues can be definitions, synonyms, antonyms, or a sentence with the answer left out.

5. Have your child make a second copy of the grid, leaving out the answers to make a blank puzzle.

6. Give the clues and blank puzzle to a family member. Invite your child to help him or her complete it.

Across
1. A genie grants them to you.
5. Opposite of *out*.
6. When you win something by chance.
7. "Please lock the _____."
9. The "legs" of a car.

Down
1. It's made of glass and you look out of it.
2. Same as 5 across.
3. Second, minute, _____.
4. "For goodness _____!"
6. How you feel when you care for someone very much.
8. Nickname for *Alan*.

Parent Letters for the Primary Grades ©1997 Creative Teaching Press

Dear Parents,

Did You Know?

Learning that words have meaning and are connected to ideas is an important language-arts skill. To help your child make the word/meaning connection, invite him or her to "play" with words. One way to play with words is to write them and illustrate their meaning through the way letters are made. To give it a try, have your child make some Picture Words like those described below. It's a creative and meaningful to improve your child's vocabulary!

How You Can Help

1. Gather art supplies such as paper, crayons, markers, paint, and chalk.

2. Help your child choose four or five words he or she would like to illustrate. Some easy-to-picture words include *tight, tall, wide, hole, fire, ladder, rainbow, love,* and *cloud.* Neatly print the words on paper.

3. Have your child describe the meaning of each word. Encourage your child to give examples of objects that describe the word or experiences he or she has had with them.

4. Invite your child to write each word, designing the letters so they show the word's meaning. (See the illustration for ideas.)

5. Display the words for everyone to admire.

Dear Parents,

Did You Know?

Your child builds his or her vocabulary by hearing new words on a regular basis. When your child hears new words often, they lose their "newness" and become comfortable for him or her to say, write, and read. A fun way to help your child learn new words is to have your family play Big Word of the Week. Try it—in a (big) word, it's fantastic!

How You Can Help

1. Help your child think of a word he or she uses several times a day, such as *tired, thirsty, bored, fun,* or *hungry.*

2. Think of a "big word" that means the same thing as the word your child chose, such as *famished* for *hungry.*

3. Write the original word on a large piece of paper and draw an X through it. Next to the original word, write the new word. Post the paper on a refrigerator or door.

4. Inform the family that, for a week, no one is allowed to say the original word *(hungry).* Instead, they must replace it with the new word *(famished).*

5. Have family members try to catch each other saying the banned word and then remind the rule-breaker of the new word.

6. Invite your child to pick a new word each week.

Parent Letters for the Primary Grades ©1997 Creative Teaching Press

Dear Parents,

Did You Know?

If you tell family stories and respond to your child's questions about your family's past, you encourage your child's curiosity about history and build his or her sense of identity and self-esteem. Old photographs are a perfect springboard for family-history discussions. Use an old photograph and A Moment in the Life to peak your child's curiosity about family history and help answer the question, *What makes me special?*

How You Can Help

1. With your child, go through the picture collection of an older relative and choose at least one photo of a family member (taken before your child's birth).

2. Explain where and when the picture was taken.

3. Tell your child the approximate age of the person in the picture.

4. Explain how old you were and where your family lived at the time the picture was taken.

5. While looking through the pictures, point out any differences in clothing, furniture, or hairstyles compared to today.

6. Ask your child to tell how the person (and the family) has changed since the picture was taken. Have him or her share what has stayed the same.

7. Invite the relative to talk with your child, share a family story, and tell him or her how life has changed since that time.

Parent Letters for the Primary Grades ©1997 Creative Teaching Press

Dear Parents,

Did You Know?

When your child chronicles his or her life, he or she sees the importance of being a unique individual and part of your family. A natural time for personal chronicling is on your child's birthday. Help your child gather his or her past-year memories and photos in a birthday album. Then, each year, add to the album until your child is grown. He or she will love making the album and cherish it always.

How You Can Help

1. Gather a photo album, scissors, writing paper, and pens. If you wish, include page decorations such as stickers, rubber stamps, cutouts, and colored paper.

2. Have your child look through photos of him- or herself starting from age one to the present.

3. Invite your child to choose two or three favorite photos from each year.

4. Have your child place each year's photos on one page of the album and write a short description of the events or experiences.

5. At the top of each page, have your child write his or her age at the time the photos were taken.

6. Ask your child to position the descriptions on the page and add any page decorations he or she wishes.

7. When the book is caught up to the present, wait one year and work on the book on your child's next birthday. On your child's birthday, have him or her add favorite past-year photos and memories to the album. Continue the tradition until your child is grown.

Parent Letters for the Primary Grades ©1997 Creative Teaching Press

Dear Parents,

Did You Know?

When your child celebrates his or her family, he or she feels connected to it, and in turn, has a greater understanding and acceptance of different families. Help your child learn to understand families by creating a A-Year-in-the-Life-of-Our-Family scrapbook. Read the following activity directions to get your child started!

How You Can Help

1. Gather a scrapbook, scissors, writing paper, tape, and pens. If you wish, include decorations such as stickers, rubber stamps, cutouts, and colored paper.

2. Have your child hunt through drawers, baskets, photo albums, and boxes to find small objects and photos that symbolize experiences your family had in the past year. (Objects could include bumper stickers, key chains, souvenirs, tickets, or tags.)

3. Gather the family. Invite them to glue or tape the photos and objects onto scrapbook pages and attach written explanations of experiences represented by them. Have your child add decorations if he or she wishes.

4. As a family, read the scrapbook.

5. Create a new scrapbook once a year on a designated day such as New Year's Day.

Dear Parents,

Did You Know?

History is best learned by hearing stories about people. One of the best ways to teach your child history and appreciation for others is to tell him or her stories about very familiar people—members of your own family! Choose a special time and complete the Family Stories activity. Your child will learn history, and best of all, respect for those who came before him or her.

How You Can Help

1. Once a year, gather extended and immediate family members. (Holidays such as Thanksgiving are a perfect time!)

2. At the beginning of the day, ask each person to think of one "historical story" he or she would like to tell about the family. Explain that stories can be about ancestors, family members at the gathering, or him- or herself.

3. Include all family members in storytelling, even the youngest.

4. At the end of the day, have everyone sit together and share stories.

5. Continue the tradition every year.

Parent Letters for the Primary Grades ©1997 Creative Teaching Press

Dear Parents,

Did You Know?

High self-esteem can help your child succeed in and out of school. Help your child develop self-esteem by talking with him or her every day, reading to him or her, and engaging him or her in special projects. One special self-esteem-building project is creating an Alphabet Memory Book. Make one with your child to remember always.

How You Can Help

1. Gather 13 pieces of drawing paper. Have your child use crayons or markers to label the fronts and backs of each page with a letter of the alphabet. For example, write *A* on the front of a page and *B* on the back.

2. Invite your child to think of a special memory that begins with each letter, such as C *is for camping.*

3. Have your child write about the memory by completing the following sentence pattern: ___ *is for* _____ *because* _____. For example, C *is for camping because we go every year.*

4. Invite your child to use crayons, markers, colored pencils, or paint to illustrate each page.

5. Using string, brads, or staples, bind the pages inside a cardboard book cover. Have your child write *Alphabet Memory Book* on the cover and decorate it.

6. Place the book on your coffee table or bookshelf for all to share.

Dear Parents,

Did You Know?

Television programs and movies offer loads of historical information. The key to turning programs and movies into educational tools is to have meaningful discussion before and after your child sees them. To get started, use Children Long Ago and Today with your child.

How You Can Help

1. Help your child list all the things he or she does in one day, such as go to school, play, do chores, eat, and sleep.

2. Discuss the list, asking your child to describe each action in detail.

3. Watch a movie together that shows the life of a pioneer child, such as *Little House on the Prairie* or *Old Yeller.* Ask your child to look for examples from the list in the movie.

4. After watching, invite your child to reread the list he or she made.

5. Ask your child to tell how his or her actions on the list differ from those of pioneer children. Have your child give examples from the movie.

6. Invite your child to ask any questions about machines, clothing, events, or practices he or she noticed in the movie. If you do not know the answers, find them together.

Parent Letters for the Primary Grades ©1997 Creative Teaching Press

Dear Parents,

Did You Know?

When your child knows about global and local events, he or she learns about history, politics, and human nature at the same time. To help your child focus on the positive side of human nature, discuss "good news" in news reports as often as "bad news." To get started, use Good News described below—it'll help your child put the world's events in perspective.

How You Can Help

1. Discuss the need for good news in today's news reports.

2. With your child, read the headlines from world, national, and local news sections.

3. Invite your child to circle each headline that gives good news, such as news of peace, a scientific breakthrough, or a successful event.

4. Have your child choose three articles in which he or she is most interested. Read the articles to your child and discuss them.

5. Ask your child to choose his or her favorite article and explain why.

6. Together, write a letter to the newspaper commending them for reporting good news. Have your child refer to the article and tell why he or she liked it.

7. Send the letter. Explain that even if you do not receive a reply, you have learned something and promoted the reporting of good news.

Dear Parents,

Did You Know?

You can make the "whole-wide world" seem a little smaller and a little more real to your child. Whenever possible, discuss the news—especially events that take place outside of your community. Help your child gain a greater understanding of the world by discussing the interdependence of all countries. A great way to begin is to use Today's News—soon your child will have the world at his or her fingertips.

How You Can Help

1. Read a daily newspaper, or listen to or watch a news report with your child.

2. Choose a foreign country featured in a report and point it out on a map.

3. Help your child understand how far away the country is by discussing how you could travel there and how long it would take. If you wish, consult an atlas or encyclopedia to calculate the exact distance.

4. Ask your child if he or she thinks the news event will affect your country in any way. Discuss possible connections with your country.

5. To find an answer (and demonstrate how events in one country affect another), make a line across your kitchen with string. Call one side of the line *Bubbleland* and the other *Nobubbles*.

6. Give your child a bottle of blowing bubbles. Ask your child to imagine the bubbles are pollution.

7. Invite your child to sit in Bubbleland and blow the bubbles toward Nobubbles. Discuss how the people in Nobubbles might feel if a lot of bubbles came into their country. Relate the activity to the news event you discussed.

Parent Letters for the Primary Grades © 1997 Creative Teaching Press

Dear Parents,

Did You Know?

Part of understanding history is knowing which events, people, and items are from the present, recent past, or distant past. Your child's perspective of the distant past may be different from yours, but accept his or her ideas—your child is learning the concept of time as it relates to his or her own age. To give your child some historical-age practice, invite him or her to place items into categories by playing Old, Older, Oldest.

How You Can Help

1. Gather several household items and photographs. Make sure to include some new, old, and very-old items.

2. Explain that you are going to place some household items into categories.

3. Call category one *Our Times*. These are times you and your child can both remember. Call category two *Before My Time*. These are times from your birth to your child's. Call category three *Long Ago*. These are times before your birth.

4. Help your child make a three-section sorting tray, shelf, or mat. (See the illustration for ideas.) Label each section with a category.

5. Display the household items, and have your child think about each and place each item in a category on the mat.

6. When your child suggests an inappropriate place for an item, tell him or her the item's "story" to help with its placement.

Dear Parents,

Did You Know?

Most museums have curators who take care of and catalog artifacts. Curators also know the stories (or histories) of the items and have studied subjects related to them. Your child can learn what a curator does and about the process of studying history by putting together his or her own mini museum.

How You Can Help

1. Find a place that can become a mini-museum display, such as a shelf or table.

2. Have your child think of "long-ago artifacts" he or she wants to feature by choosing a theme such as articles from babyhood or your childhood. (If your household has very few "long-ago artifacts," arrange a visit to an older relative or friend and borrow some.)

3. Invite your child to collect and display the items in the designated area for a museum opening.

4. Help your child make labels for the items. Labels should include descriptions of people, places, events, and a general time frame. Your child may also want to name his or her display and label it with a sign.

5. For the opening, invite your child to become the museum guide and explain each item or make a tape-recorded guide for visitors.

6. For future exhibits, have your child borrow items from family members, just like real museums do. (They borrow from private individuals and from other museums.) Explain the borrowing practice and ask why he or she thinks museums borrow artifacts.

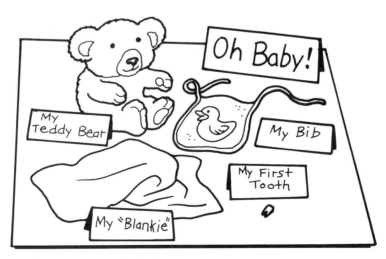

Parent Letters for the Primary Grades ©1997 Creative Teaching Press

Dear Parents,

Did You Know?

Relief maps are maps with raised and lowered areas to show the altitude of the earth. On relief maps, mountains and volcanoes are raised and oceans and canyons are lowered. Relief maps are children's favorites because they are "hands-on," offering them something to touch. Have your child create a relief map—it's a creative and fun way to learn!

How You Can Help

1. Gather a large plywood square, a permanent marker, modeling clay that hardens, tempera paints, and paintbrushes.

2. Describe relief maps and their purpose. With your child, visit a library or school to observe several relief maps.

3. First, invite your child to draw an aerial view of an imaginary land. Be sure to have your child include mountains, rivers that connect to lakes, volcanoes, and any other land formations he or she chooses.

4. Once the drawing is complete, have your child transfer it to plywood using permanent marker.

5. Invite your child to use modeling clay and create raised areas to show the altitude of the map's land formations. After the clay dries, have your child paint the map.

6. Discuss the map with your child. Have your child explain why each land formation is placed in its location. After discussion, invite him or her to play with the map using toy cars, boats, dolls, and buildings for hours of creative play.

Geography

Dear Parents,

Did You Know?

The seven largest land masses on Earth are called continents. The continents include Africa, Antarctica, Asia, Australia, Europe, North America, and South America. Children sometimes confuse continents and countries (Australia is both). To help your child understand the concept of continents (and countries, states, cities, and neighborhoods), do the following activity—he or she will gain a world of knowledge!

How You Can Help

1. Find a world map (with continents and countries marked), your country's map (with states or provinces marked), a state or province map (with cities and towns marked), and a map of your community.

2. Review the community map with your child. Invite your child to place a marker, such as a penny, near your street. Discuss the size of your community and which other communities it borders. Ask your child if he or she thinks your community is larger than your state/province. (You might be surprised at the answer.)

3. Review the state/province map with your child. Help him or her find your community (or one near it), and mark it. Compare the size of your state/province to that of your community. Discuss your state's/province's size and others it borders. Ask your child if he or she thinks your state/province is larger than your country.

4. Review the country map with your child. Help your child find your state/province, and mark it. Compare the size of your country to that of your state/province. Discuss your country's size and the countries it borders. Ask your child if he or she thinks your country is larger than the continent on which it lies.

5. Using the world map, point out your country and have your child mark it. Compare the size of your country to that of its continent. Discuss your continent and those connected to it.

Parent Letters for the Primary Grades ©1997 Creative Teaching Press

Dear Parents,

Did You Know?

Compass points (north, south, east, west, and variations of these four directions) are an important part of geography. They help people read maps and find destinations. To help your child become familiar with compass points, play Simon Says as described below. Your child will learn about geography and gain a better sense of direction.

How You Can Help

1. Using a compass, help your child find the north side of the room.

2. Remind your child that the sun rises in the east and sets in the west. Have him or her use the compass and identify those directions. Finally, point out south.

3. Play Simon Says, giving commands such as *Simon says, take two steps to the east,* or *Simon says, take one step to the south.*

4. Switch places and let your child be Simon.

5. Lead your child to another room in the house to play again.

6. When your child can play well, place a large map on the wall and have your child locate north, south, east, and west by using his or her fingers to trace and obey Simon's commands. Choose a starting point on the map and invite your child to place his or her index finger on it. When Simon says to go north, have your child move his or her finger up the map. His or her finger should move down for south, left for west, and right for east.

Geography

Dear Parents,

Did You Know?

Locating places on a map often calls for finding coordinates. (For example, a map index may say, *Roger Street (L, 12)*. Roger Street would be in the square formed by the intersection of map sections *L* and *12*. Use Plot a Picture to give your child practice with coordinates. His or her coordinate skills will soon be "on the mark."

How You Can Help

1. Using the attached grid, invite your child to find the point *E,3*. Help him or her if needed.

2. Have your child find *J,3*, and connect the two points with a straight line.

3. Continue with the following pairs, encouraging your child to connect the points after each new one is added: *J,3/L,5; L,5/C,5; C,5/E,3; G,5/G,11; G,11/B,6;* and *B,6/G,6*.

4. When all dots are connected, your child should get a picture of a sailboat.

5. Using the same-size grid, invite your child to draw his or her own original coordinate picture and then tell you coordinates so you can make a copy.

6. As your child progresses, provide smaller-squared graph paper.

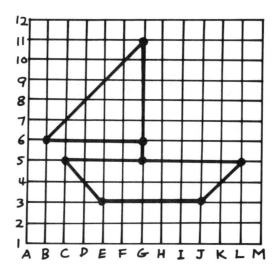

Parent Letters for the Primary Grades © 1997 Creative Teaching Press

Plot a Picture

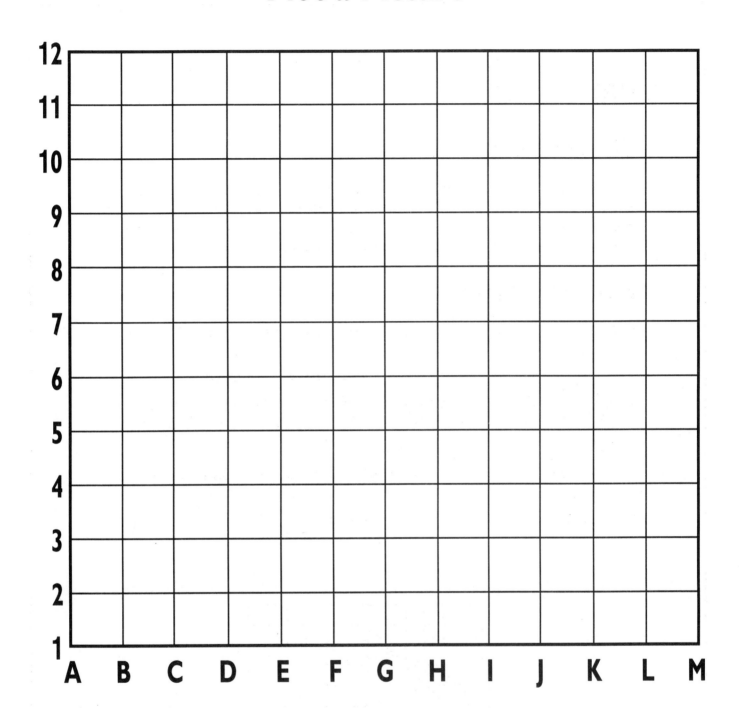

Geography

Dear Parents,

Did You Know?

Part of geography is learning direction. Before *north, south, east,* and *west,* your child needs to learn words such as *left, right, up, down,* and *in front of* or *in back of* when giving directions. These words give your child powerful tools for describing location. Play Radar Words to help your child work with direction vocabulary—this game is right on target!

How You Can Help

1. Play this variation of 20 Questions to strengthen your child's understanding of directional words. To begin, have your child choose a mystery object in plain sight.

2. Ask questions that pinpoint the location of the object, such as *Is it above my head? Is it on the left side of the room? Is it next to the chair? Is it to the right of the television?* Use directional words and phrases such as *up, down, above, on top of, below, higher, lower, behind,* and *in front of.*

3. After you name the object, have your child become the guesser.

4. When your child is comfortable giving directions, label the room *north, south, east,* and *west,* and use those terms in your questions.

Parent Letters for the Primary Grades © 1997 Creative Teaching Press

Dear Parents,

Did You Know?

With knowledge of communities, your child learns about how people live—their transportation, occupations, and culture—as well as geography and directional skills. You can build your child's knowledge of communities by helping him or her learn about neighborhoods. Activities like Street Smart will give your child social-studies and real-world skills (like finding his or her way home).

How You Can Help

1. Choose a neighborhood and take a walk with your child.

2. Invite your child to look for street names that fit into groups such as names of trees, presidents, or numbers. Look for patterns in the names and ask your child how the patterns make it easier for strangers to find their way.

3. Read aloud a building's address. Walk farther and read a second address. Ask your child which way you would have to walk to get to an address lower or higher than those passed. (For example, ask, *If the first address is 200 and this one is 202, would you continue in the same direction or turn around to get to 194?*)

4. Invite your child to count numbers on each side of the street. Point out the pattern—odd numbers on one side and even numbers on the other.

5. Explain that in some parts of the world, people do not use street numbers and names, but people still get their mail. Explain why—buildings don't change much, people don't move often, populations are small, and houses are spread out.

6. Find out if the neighborhood has a name. Discuss possible reasons for the name. If possible, discover the name's origin.

Dear Parents,

Did You Know?

Each community has something unique to offer. Sometimes it's hidden, but with a little looking, you and your child can find it. Even places such as a food store, post office, hospital, municipal building, public-transportation terminal, bank, auto repair shop, or animal shelter can offer interesting insights. Use Around-Town Tourist to help you arrange a behind-the-scenes tour of a place in your community.

How You Can Help

1. Choose a place in your community your child might enjoy visiting. Ask your child about the destination to find out what he or she knows.

2. With your child, develop a list of questions to be answered on the trip. Develop answer-getting strategies such as watching carefully, reading posted information, and talking to workers.

3. Go on the tour. As your child explores the site, look for people, activities, and equipment that he or she wants to discuss and draw (or photograph).

4. If possible, take a camera and have your child shoot some photos. (Before the trip, discuss "photo courtesy"—asking people for permission before taking photos.)

5. After the tour, ask your child to tell his or her favorite and least-favorite parts.

6. With drawing paper and art supplies, have your child make an illustrated guide book with one-sentence captions near drawings or attached photos.

7. Help your child write and send thank-you notes to helpful people from the tour.

Parent Letters for the Primary Grades © 1997 Creative Teaching Press

Dear Parents,

Did You Know?

Your community offers dozens of opportunities to teach your child social studies. Local museums offer a glimpse into history. Monuments and town squares help your child understand the community's roots. Community maps help your child learn the concepts of direction, size, and distance. When using a local map, refer to Our Town described below. It'll help your child "find the way" to community understanding.

How You Can Help

1. Obtain a detailed map of your community. (If you do not have one, ask your public librarian for one to copy.) Make several copies to keep for later use.

2. Mark your home on the map with your child.

3. Mark other landmarks your child knows, such as his or her school, a shopping area, friends' or relatives' streets, or your workplace.

4. Trace routes you have taken together to reach the marked places. Discuss landmarks seen along the way and the time each trip takes walking or by car.

5. When tracing streets on the map, discuss significant street names such as those named after community leaders or founders.

6. Keep another map in the car. Each time you take a familiar or new route, invite your child to trace it with his or her finger on the map.

Communities

Dear Parents,

Did You Know?

When your child understands that all communities are interdependent, he or she gains a greater appreciation for communities and cultures different from his or her own. Two things all communities have in common are the need for food and the capacity to grow it. Because of this supply and demand, the whole world depends on each other through importing and exporting food. The following activity helps your child understand this interdependence.

How You Can Help

1. With your child, read labels from several canned, packaged, and refrigerated foods.

2. Help your child read manufacturers' and distributors' names to find each food's place of origin. (Explain *distributor*—a company that buys goods from farmers or manufacturers and resells them to stores.)

3. Help your child make two lists, one of locations within your country and one of foreign locations.

4. Using your country's map, move your finger from each food company's location to your community. Discuss how food might be transported and kept fresh.

5. For imported foods, locate food companies' locations on a world map and trace each to your community. Discuss food transportation and freshness control.

The oranges from Florida go by truck to Tennessee.

Parent Letters for the Primary Grades ©1997 Creative Teaching Press

Dear Parents,

Did You Know?

Throughout school, your child will learn to read maps, their symbols, and legends (keys). One of the first maps your child will see in school (and places such as zoos and amusements parks) is a picture map. Picture maps use icons and illustrations to show destinations. Help your child learn about picture maps and your community by doing Make a Map with him or her.

How You Can Help

1. Invite your child to quickly sketch a picture map that shows the route from your home to school, a friend's house, or another place he or she chooses.

2. Take a camera, and walk the route with your child. Invite your child to take snapshots of easy-to-spot landmarks along the way.

3. After the photos are developed, have your child use a large piece of paper to make a new map by drawing each photographed landmark in sequence. Have your child add color to the map with crayons or markers.

4. Have your child compare the original map to the new one. Ask him or her which map is more accurate and detailed.

5. Discuss map makers (cartographers). Have your child think about his or her map-making experience and tell what map makers probably do to make accurate maps.

6. Test the new map by asking another family member to use it and find his or her way to the destination.

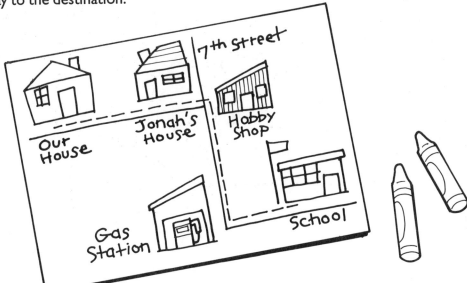

Dear Parents,

Did You Know?

Plant scientists sort, categorize, and name every new plant species they find. Classifying living things establishes order and helps scientists find similarities and differences between the objects they study. Your child can become a "scientific sorter" by observing and classifying leaves he or she finds on a walk.

How You Can Help

1. Take a walk with your child, and encourage him or her to collect one leaf from each different kind of tree you see.

2. Each time your child picks up a leaf, invite him or her to tell you how it is different from those already collected.

3. Spread out the collection when you get home.

4. Without telling your child how you divided them, separate the leaves into two groups. For example, group red leaves and non-red leaves. Other categories might include ragged-edge/smooth-edge, needles/no needles, or thin/wide.

5. Invite your child to guess the sorting rule used to classify the leaves.

6. Next, have your child sort the leaves. Guess his or her sorting rule.

7. Take turns until you run out of ideas. Play sorting games with other natural objects such as flowers or insect and animal pictures.

Parent Letters for the Primary Grades ©1997 Creative Teaching Press

Dear Parents,

Did You Know?

Scientific observation requires us to see, hear, touch, taste, and smell to gather as much information as possible. To help your child understand more about his or her body and the practice of scientific observation, have him or her play Sensory Sit Down. It's "Sense-ational"!

How You Can Help

1. Take your child to a room where only background noise can be heard.

2. Hide a few objects in the room that appeal to your child's senses. Be sure some objects are soft, scratchy, strong-smelling, and safe for your child to taste.

3. Invite your child to close his or her eyes and listen. Ask your child to tell what sounds he or she hears, the rooms from which they come, and their source.

4. Encourage your child (with eyes closed) to touch his or her hands, face, and clothing. Say, *Rub your fingertips together. Gently touch your hair and your face. Touch your clothing.* Have your child describe what he or she feels.

5. One at a time, hand your child the hidden objects. Ask your child to describe how each feels and guess its identity.

6. Next, have your child use the sense of smell. Ask your child to describe anything he or she can smell. Have your child sniff other objects, describe them, and guess their identity.

7. Have your child use the sense of taste and repeat the activity.

8. Ask your child to open his or her eyes and slowly observe the room. Invite him or her to focus on different shapes, colors, and sizes, looking for repeated patterns. Have your child give a detailed description of each item he or she sees.

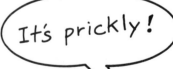

It's prickly!

Dear Parents,

Did You Know?

Every animal has food preferences and each specie's body is adapted to eat the kinds of food it likes. Your child can learn about adaptations and food preferences by watching birds in your own backyard. Have your child use For the Birds to get started.

How You Can Help

1. Give your child three large pinecones and three pieces of string.

2. Supply three different foods (such as bread crumbs, raisins, popcorn, or pieces of fruit). Your child will discover which types of foods appeal to different birds.

3. Mix peanut butter with each food, and stuff each mixture between a pinecone's spines.

4. Hang the pinecone feeders from an easily-observed high spot (safe from cats).

5. Have your child watch the feeders for several days and keep a record of which birds visit. Soon your child will discover specific birds' food preferences.

6. As your child observes each bird, have him or her describe the bird's beak. Ask your child why he or she thinks the bird has a particular-shaped beak (to eat the kind of food it likes).

7. After observation, invite your child to choose his or her favorite bird and create and hang bird feeders with its favorite meal so they will visit again and again.

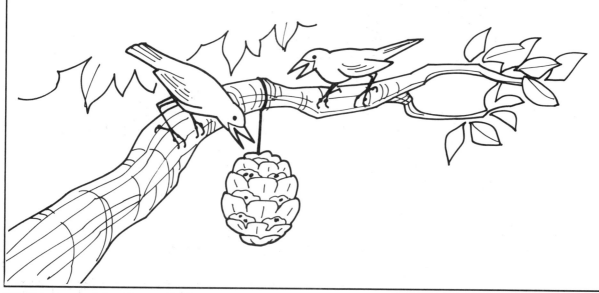

Parent Letters for the Primary Grades ©1997 Creative Teaching Press

Dear Parents,

Did You Know?

Nature offers your child the perfect opportunity to use and learn about his or her five senses. Your child can be just like scientists and "take to the field," observing things in their natural habitat. To help your child learn how his or her body works when making observations, use Making Sense Outside. It makes nature walks more interesting and science more fun!

How You Can Help

1. Take your child on several walks around the neighborhood, each time concentrating on a different sense.

2. On smell or sound walks, hold your child's hand while he or she walks wearing a blindfold to focus closely on sounds or smells.

3. On touch walks, have your child use crayons and paper to make rubbings of textured objects. (Make rubbings by having your child place paper over an object and rub with the flat side of a crayon.)

4. On sight walks, have your child use a camera or drawing materials to record what he or she sees underfoot and overhead.

Life Science and the Human Body

Dear Parents,

Did You Know?

Strenuous exercise requires a lot of oxygen from your body's cells. To get the oxygen it needs during exercise, blood is sent quickly through your body, causing your heart rate to quicken. Your child can experience the effect of exercise on heart rate by completing Pulse-Rate Predictions—it's a good workout, too!

How You Can Help

1. Help your child list five physical activities he or she could do in 30 seconds, such as sit-ups, jumping rope, walking around the room, running in place, and jumping jacks. Have your child predict and list the activities from least strenuous to most strenuous.

2. Help your child take his or her resting pulse. (Find the pulse as shown in the illustration, count the beats for 15 seconds, and multiply that number by four.)

3. Starting with the least strenuous activity, have your child do each and write down his or her pulse rate after completion.

4. Before beginning a new activity, have your child rest until his or her pulse rate comes down to the resting rate. Ask your child to test his or her pulse rate for each activity.

5. Invite your child to look at his or her written record and decide if the guesses were correct.

6. Explain why the heartbeat speeds up during exercise.

Parent Letters for the Primary Grades © 1997 Creative Teaching Press

Dear Parents,

Did You Know?

Plant roots are like veins—they carry water and nutrients from the soil to the rest of the plant. You can demonstrate how roots pick up water and nutrients from the soil by doing Root Canals with your child. He or she will have a better understanding of soil and plants as well as why fertilizer goes into the soil rather than on the plant.

How You Can Help

1. Split a celery stalk (with leaves) from bottom to top, leaving the top joined. Explain that the celery stalk represents a plant in soil.

2. Place one piece of stalk into a glass with 1/4 cup water and 1/2 teaspoon red food coloring. Explain that the water represents water in the soil and the food coloring represents the soil's nutrients.

3. Place the other piece into 1/4 cup water and 1/2 teaspoon blue food coloring.

4. After half an hour, invite your child to observe the celery.

5. Point out the color of the narrow tubes running up the stalks. Explain that these are like a plant's root system, carrying nutrients and water to all plant parts.

6. Explain that underground, roots take nutrients and water from the soil and send them to the rest of the plant to help it grow.

Dear Parents,

Did You Know?

The pulse on your wrist is the rhythmic throbbing of your arteries as they carry blood away from your heart and through your body. The arteries throb because your heart pumps the blood and causes pressure. A pulse measures your heart rate and can tell doctors approximately how fast your heart is beating and how hard it is working.

How You Can Help

1. Provide your child with a small scoop of modeling clay and a toothpick or small straw piece.

2. Locate your child's pulse by placing your index and middle fingers on opposite sides of your child's wrist next to the base of his or her hand. Press lightly until you can feel the pulse.

3. Invite your child to place a piece of clay on the spot where the pulse is strongest.

4. Flatten out the clay and place the straw or toothpick in it.

5. Have your child lay his or her arm on a flat surface and watch the straw or toothpick move with each beat.

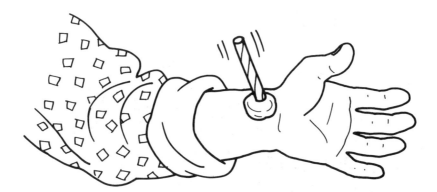

Parent Letters for the Primary Grades ©1997 Creative Teaching Press

Dear Parents,

Did You Know?

The beating sound made by the heart is produced by opening and closing valves. The moving valves help blood circulate from the heart, to the lungs, back to the heart, and through the body. While in the body, blood gives your cells oxygen and food nutrients. Your child can listen to your heart valves open and close by making a homemade stethoscope. Try this fun, "hearty" activity today!

How You Can Help

1. Provide your child with a 15-inch rubber or plastic tube and a pair of funnels.

2. Invite your child to fit the narrow end of each funnel into opposite ends of the tubing.

3. Ask your child to put one funnel over your heart and the other to his or her ear, and listen to your heartbeat.

4. Show your child a heart diagram, point out the valves, and discuss what causes heartbeats and how and why the heart pumps blood.

Dear Parents,

Did You Know?

Jets and race cars and are sleekly designed to increase speed by reducing wind resistance. Parachutes and gliders have a wide-open design to do the opposite. They increase wind resistance to slow the effect of gravity and float slowly to the ground. Have your child learn about wind resistance by making his or her own "sky diver."

How You Can Help

1. Provide your child with a clothespin (the kind you push instead of pinch).

2. Invite your child to make a sky diver by drawing a face on the clothespin and decorating it to look like a person. Have him or her add yarn hair and cloth-scrap clothing.

3. For a first launch, ask your child to predict what will happen if he or she throws the clothespin high in the air. Invite your child to try it. Use a watch with a second hand to time the landing.

4. For the second launch, tie a piece of string to each corner of a handkerchief parachute. Tie the loose ends of the strings around the clothespin's "neck."

5. Ask your child what he or she thinks will happen when the clothespin is thrown in the air again. Have your child launch the clothespin. Time the landing.

6. Ask your child why the clothespin took longer to land the second time. Add scientific vocabulary to your child's description by explaining wind resistance.

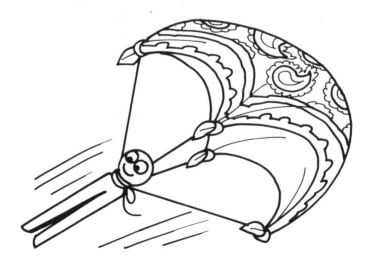

Parent Letters for the Primary Grades © 1997 Creative Teaching Press

Dear Parents,

Did You Know?

The faster air moves, the less pressure (or pushing down) it creates. For example, air that flows over airplane wings moves faster and pushes down on the plane less than the air that flows under the wings. This lack of pressure causes the plane to lift off the ground. Help your child learn about and demonstrate this principle by using Blow to Know—it's an "uplifting" experience!

How You Can Help

1. Give your child a 4" x 6" (10 cm x 15 cm) piece of paper, and pretend it is an airplane wing.

2. Ask your child to hold it just under his or her bottom lip, letting the paper sag.

3. Have your child blow out a stream of air and observe what happens to the paper (it lifts up).

4. Ask your child why he or she thinks the paper flutters up and not down. Explain the concept of air pressure as it relates to fast-moving air.

5. For more information on flight and air pressure, consult an encyclopedia, and invite your child to check out airplane books from the library.

Physical Science

Dear Parents,

Did You Know?

Humidity (the amount of moisture in the air) is a term your child will learn when studying the properties of water. One property of water is evaporation—when heated water molecules turn into steam, float, and enter the air, causing humidity. To help your child understand how humidity causes objects to expand, use The Incredible Growing Drawer.

How You Can Help

1. On a humid day, have your child open and close all wooden drawers in your house and notice how smoothly they glide. Ask, *Do the drawers glide quickly? Do you hear a noise when opening and closing the drawers? Do any drawers stick?*

2. When your child encounters a sticky/noisy drawer, explain that the day is humid. Discuss how on a humid day, there is a lot of water in the air. The water wants to find a place to land so it is taken in (absorbed) by the wood from the drawers. This causes the drawer to get bigger (expand), just like a dry sponge that "fattens up" when it takes in water. Tell your child that the bigger-sized drawer is harder to fit in the slot, so it sticks and makes noise.

3. Invite your child to look for others signs of humidity, such as steam; fog on windows and mirrors; and creaking, hard-to-shut doors.

Dear Parents,

Did You Know?

In science, a physical change occurs when two or more items are combined but do not cause a chemical reaction and become a new substance. For example, with Kool-aid, the sugar and flavoring dissolve in the water, but the water remains water and can be removed from the mixture through evaporation. As with Kool-aid, your child can practice making physical changes using food.

How You Can Help

1. Place a scoop of white frosting on a graham cracker.

2. Discuss physical changes and explain that you will be making one today.

3. Invite your child to add a drop of food coloring to the frosting, and mix the color on the graham cracker. Ask, *Did the color change anything about the frosting's smell, texture, or taste? Did the frosting change into something new or did it remain frosting?* Remind your child that a physical change means nothing new was created.

4. Invite your child to eat his or her "changed" graham cracker!

Dear Parents,

Did You Know?

Molecules are tiny pieces of matter that, when hooked together, make up everything around us. Water is made of connected molecules. Water molecules become "slippery" when soap is added to them, loosening the molecules' connections. When water molecules are slippery, they spread apart. The following activity helps your child understand that molecules are connected and that their connections can be loosened.

How You Can Help

1. Fill a clean pie pan with cold water.

2. When the water is still, lightly sprinkle talcum powder over the surface. The powder should stay on top. Explain that the tiny parts (molecules) that make up water are "holding hands" (connected), holding the powder in place.

3. Place a drop of liquid soap at the water's edge. (The powder will shoot away.)

4. Explain that the soap made the water "slippery" and caused the "holding hands" to weaken their grip. The looser grip made the water droplets spread apart (like loosening hands) and move the powder. Explain that the moving powder shows that the water's tiny parts (molecules) are loosened and can move.

Parent Letters for the Primary Grades ©1997 Creative Teaching Press

Dear Parents,

Did You Know?

All matter has mass (similar to weight) and takes up space. Air, although invisible, is matter that takes up space. For example, a balloon shows that air, upon entering the balloon, takes up space by making the balloon bigger. Try an experiment with your child and help him or her understand that air is matter and takes up space.

How You Can Help

1. Open a can of liquid by punching a hole in the side of the can's lid.

2. Have your child pour the liquid into another container, noticing the speed with which the liquid comes out.

3. With the can still partly full, punch a second hole in the other side of the lid. Invite your child to pour again and notice the liquid's speed. Ask your child why he or she thinks the liquid pours faster with two holes.

4. Explain that with only one hole, the air outside the can takes up space and pushes against the liquid coming out and slows it down. With two holes, air enters the can and takes the place of the liquid leaving it. The air inside of the can causes pressure and helps push the remaining liquid out.

Dear Parents,

Did You Know?

Heat (from the sun, your house's heater or oven, or any other source) causes air to expand. When air expands, it becomes lighter. As heated (lighter) air rises, cooler (heavier) air moves in to take its place. When this occurs, wind is created. Help your child understand what causes wind by finding examples in your home—he or she will be "blown away"!

How You Can Help

1. Explain that wind is caused by the movement of warm and cool air when they meet.

2. Have your child choose several places in your house where he or she thinks warm and cool air meet, such as window edges, door bottoms, or openings to attics or basements.

3. Ask your child which place is windiest. Light a piece of incense and have your child place it in each chosen spot.

4. Have your child notice the speed and direction of the smoke in the windiest place.

5. On the next windy day, remind your child of the movement when warm and cool air meet. (If the day is warm or cool, have your child predict what the weather will be the next day—probably the opposite.)

Parent Letters for the Primary Grades ©1997 Creative Teaching Press

Dear Parents,

Did You Know?

The earth is constantly changing for your child to see. He or she can learn about the changing earth and its weather, water, shape, and erosion simply by observing rainy-day running water and puddles. Try Pondering Puddles—it's a fun, easy way to make rainy days exciting!

How You Can Help

1. Take a walk in the rain with your child. Bring a yardstick and a tape measure.

2. Look for places to observe running water (a force in nature that wears down the earth's surface). Look for areas with bare soil and have your child notice the color of the runoff.

3. Have your child look at running water in a grassy area. Ask your child how grass protects the soil. (Grass roots hold it in place.)

4. Explain that rivers and valleys are formed when erosion takes place. Erosion happens when running water cuts into the earth and carries away soil (just like the bare soil seen by your child). Explain how erosion can be bad for farmers upstream (it takes away topsoil rich in nutrients) and good for those downstream (it brings them rich topsoil).

5. Encourage your child to notice puddles, and ask him or her why they form in those areas. Explain that puddles form in low and eroded areas.

6. Invite your child to measure puddles to find which are longest, widest, and deepest. Ask him or her to predict which puddle will be the first and last to disappear, and if the weather has anything to do with how long the puddles stay. (Puddles evaporate faster in dry, sunny conditions.)

Earth Science

Dear Parents,

Did You Know?

The earth's surface and its rocks are changing all the time. We notice fast changes, such as those due to earthquakes and volcanoes, but are less likely to notice slow ones, such as those due to weathering and erosion. Help your child understand one way the earth changes slowly by completing Crack Me Up—he or she will never look at rocks the same way again.

How You Can Help

1. Give your child a jar. Fill it to the top with water and tightly screw on the lid.

2. Wrap a few sheets of paper towel around the jar, place the jar in a plastic bag, close the bag securely, and place it in the freezer.

3. Wait until the water is frozen solid, and then help your child carefully unwrap the jar.

4. Have your child examine the jar. (It should be broken.) Explain that the jar cracked because the water inside got bigger (expanded) as it froze.

5. Have your child imagine the jar is a large rock. Explain that freezing water also causes big rocks to crack. Water gets in the rock's cracks and expands when it freezes, causing cracks. Each time cracks fill and freeze, rocks crack even more. Over time, cracked rocks break apart and crumble. A rock may take millions of years to break completely apart because of the earth's varying weather.

Parent Letters for the Primary Grades ©1997 Creative Teaching Press

Dear Parents,

Did You Know?

The water cycle explains how water evaporates from oceans and lakes (with the sun's heat), condenses as it cools to form clouds, and (when there is enough weight in the cloud) falls to the ground as rain or snow to return to lakes and oceans. Your child will learn about the water cycle when he or she studies weather. Help your child understand the water cycle by making simple observations right in your own kitchen. Don't wait for a rainy day, try the following activity today!

How You Can Help

1. While boiling a pot of soup or water, invite your child to watch (from a distance) the steam rise into the air. Explain that as liquid heats, some of it becomes lighter and moves into the air (evaporates), and causes a cloud called *steam* (like clouds in the sky). Invite your child to look out the window at clouds. Explain that the clouds he or she sees are just large groups of water drops.

2. Ask your child what would happen if you let the pot boil a long time. Explain that the pan would burn because all the water would evaporate and move into the air.

3. Hold a metal lid to block the steam as it comes from the pot or kettle. Watch the steam condense (stick to the top of the lid) and become droplets of water that fall.

4. Explain that the falling water is just like rain. When the steam (cloud) cools (the cold lid caused it to cool quickly), it becomes heavier and falls back to earth as rain and snow.

Dear Parents,

Did You Know?

Soil needs organic matter (decayed plants and animals) rich in nutrients to encourage plant growth. Your child can help the soil by creating organic matter—compost. Add your child's compost to your houseplants, yard, and garden. Soon your plants will be "growing like weeds"!

How You Can Help

1. In a plastic container with a lid, have your child place alternate layers of fruit and vegetable waste, potting soil, leaves, and grass clippings.

2. Poke a few small holes in the lid. Have your child place the container in a sunny, outdoor location.

3. Ask your child to shake the container every other day to add air to the mixture. (If the air is warm, have your child add water to the mixture to keep it moist.)

4. After two weeks, ask your child to check the compost. (If the layered material has combined with the soil, the compost is ready.) Continue the activity if the compost is not ready.

Parent Letters for the Primary Grades ©1997 Creative Teaching Press

Dear Parents,

Did You Know?

In nature, water is cleaned as it travels through soil and rocks. Soil and rocks serve as nature's "water filter," ridding water of debris and some forms of pollution. Help your child understand the natural process of filtration by making a natural filter—it will leave him or her "thirsty" for more science.

How You Can Help

1. Explain the process of natural water filtration.

2. Using a flour sifter as a container, have your child layer absorbent cotton on top of the screening.

3. Next, have him or her layer coarse, clean sand, and then pebbles, on top of the cotton.

4. Place the filter over a bowl or wide-mouth jar.

5. Have your child pour muddy water into the filter and observe what happens.

6. Discuss filtration and how the water is cleaned as it travels through the layers. Remind your child that the water is still unsafe to drink because it probably contains invisible bacteria and chemicals.

Dear Parents,

Did You Know?

Your child will learn the scientific method during science experiments. Scientific-method steps include question (asking a scientific question), hypothesis (making a prediction about the question's answer), materials (listing materials), procedure (listing the experiment's steps), results (what happened in the experiment), and conclusion (what you learned because of the results). Use the following activity to help your child "experiment" with the scientific method.

How You Can Help

1. Ask your child the scientific question, *Does air take up space in a glass?*

2. Have your child make a hypothesis by answering *yes* or *no.*

3. Show the materials to your child—a piece of crumpled notebook paper, a drinking glass, and a container of water.

4. Push the paper into the glass bottom, and turn the glass upside-down. Have your child push it straight down into the water so water is all the way up the sides of the glass.

5. Lift the glass straight out. Have your child feel the paper. (It should be dry.) Invite your child to explain the results of the experiment.

6. Do the experiment again. This time, invite your child to tilt the glass as it is submerged. Ask your child to notice the bubbles.

7. Have your child feel the paper. (It should be wet.) Invite your child to explain the results of the second experiment.

8. To conclude, explain, *Yes, air takes up space in a glass. We know this because the first time, when you pushed the glass straight into the water, air was trapped in the upside-down glass and kept water away from the paper. The second time, air escaped from the tilted glass and water took its place, making the paper wet.*

Parent Letters for the Primary Grades ©1997 Creative Teaching Press